THE ULTIMATE
PASTA
MACHINE
COOKBOOK

THE ULTIMATE

PASTA
MACHINE
COOKBOOK

**100 RECIPES FOR
EVERY KIND OF
AMAZING PASTA
YOUR PASTA MAKER
CAN MAKE**

LUCY VASERFIRER

HARVARD
COMMON
PRESS

Brimming with creative inspiration, how-to projects, and useful information to enrich your everyday life, Quarto Knows is a favorite destination for those pursuing their interests and passions. Visit our site and dig deeper with our books into your area of interest: Quarto Creates, Quarto Cooks, Quarto Homes, Quarto Lives, Quarto Drives, Quarto Explores, Quarto Gifts, or Quarto Kids.

First Published in 2020 by The Harvard Common Press, an imprint of The Quarto Group, 100 Cummings Center, Suite 265-D, Beverly, MA 01915, USA. T (978) 282-9590 F (978) 283-2742 QuartoKnows.com

The Harvard Common Press titles are also available at discount for retail, wholesale, promotional, and bulk purchase. For details, contact the Special Sales Manager by email at specialsales@quarto.com or by mail at The Quarto Group, Attn: Special Sales Manager, 100 Cummings Center, Suite 265-D, Beverly, MA 01915, USA.

24 23 22 21 20   2 3 4 5

ISBN: 978-1-59233-948-8

Digital edition published in 2020
eISBN: 978-1-63159-877-7

Library of Congress Cataloging-in-Publication Data

Names: Vaserfirer, Lucy, author.
Title: Ultimate pasta machine cookbook : 100 recipes for every kind of
  amazing pasta your pasta maker can make / Lucy Vaserfirer.
Description: Beverly, MA : Harvard Common Press, 2020. | Includes index. |
  Summary: "With expert wisdom and a gentle, step-by-step approach, The
  Ultimate Pasta Machine Cookbook shows how to make perfect noodles in all
  kinds of shapes and flavors"-- Provided by publisher.
Identifiers: LCCN 2020002244 | ISBN 9781592339488 (trade paperback) | ISBN
  9781631598777 (ebook)
Subjects: LCSH: Cooking (Pasta) | Noodles. | Pasta machines. | LCGFT:
  Cookbooks.
Classification: LCC TX809.M17 V37 2020 | DDC 641.82/2--dc23
LC record available at https://lccn.loc.gov/2020002244

Design: Debbie Berne
Page Layout: Megan Jones Design
Photography: Lucy Vaserfirer

Printed in China

KitchenAid is a registered trademark of the Whirlpool Corporation.

For all the cooks who sink their hands into
flour and water or eggs and keep pasta
and noodle-making traditions alive.

CONTENTS

INTRODUCTION

THE PLEASURES OF PASTA

Making pasta from scratch is like alchemy or magic. Pasta is something from practically nothing, nothing but flour and water, possibly eggs. The humblest of ingredients are transformed into the most glorious of foods.

Making pasta and noodles using your pasta machine is fun, fast, and easy. It's a great outlet for your creativity, and it's incredibly satisfying both literally and figuratively—because the results are so tasty! It delights the kid in you who still loves to sink his or her fingers into playdough. It stimulates your artistic side, for each piece of pasta is an edible little sculpture. It appeals to your crafty DIY desires to create something to take pride in using your own hands. And of course, it brings out your inner chef who loves to wow friends and family with a delicious feast. What I'm saying is making pasta is a joy. The only thing that's better than making pasta is eating it!

The one and only secret to making pasta is to do it often. It's all about developing a feel for the dough. You can't really go wrong, but the more batches you have under your belt, the easier it becomes.

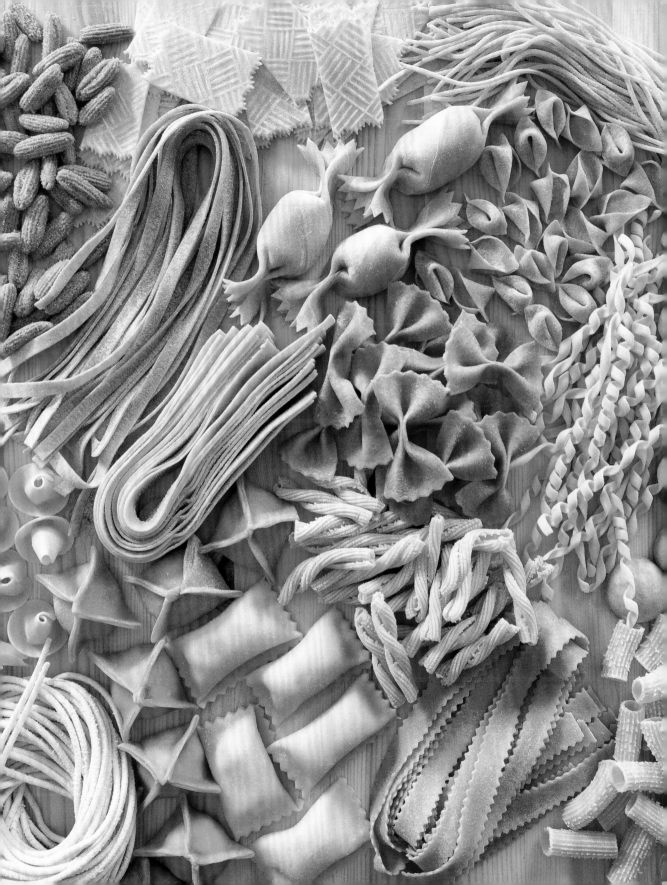

THE THREE TYPES OF PASTA MACHINES

. . . . .

THE SHEETER PASTA MACHINE

When people think of a pasta machine, they usually think of a sheeter and then an egg-and-flour dough to go along with it. As the name suggests, the sheeter transforms a mass of pasta dough into thin sheets. The dough is passed between the machine's two rollers a number of times, and the rollers are set closer and closer together with each pass. Using this machine is an alternative to the difficult and time-consuming task of sheeting dough by hand using a rolling pin, which takes years of practice to master. There are hand-crank models, electric models, and attachments for stand mixers, and they all operate the same way, though electric models are slightly easier to use.

Accessory cutters come in different sizes to make a variety of widths of pasta strands and ribbons from angel hair to pappardelle. Some give the pasta a rounded shape and some even create pasta with wavy edges. Ravioli attachments fill and mold ravioli. Also, electric motors are available for many hand-crank models.

In general, pasta made with a sheeter is the most delicate. It is silky with a lovely chew that is at once tender and resilient.

THE EXTRUDER PASTA MACHINE

An extruder forces a mass of pasta dough through a disc with holes known as a die. Most store-bought dry semolina pastas that people are familiar with such as spaghetti, linguine, fettuccine, bucatini, macaroni, rigatoni, penne, fusilli, rotini, casarecce, gemelli, and shells are actually extruded.

Most extruders, whether manual or electric, use an auger to move the dough to and through the die. Manual models such as the torchietto look almost exactly like an old-school meat grinder but have no blade. Some models have integrated mixers. As far as both manual and electric models go, the less the machine heats up the pasta as it operates, which would change the structure of the dough and even partially cook it, the better the flavor and texture of the pasta will be.

Other extruders consist of a barrel for the dough to go in with a piston to press it through the die. As far as I know these are always manual, and as you might imagine, they require a lot of muscle to operate. The Bigolaro, also known as a torchio, is the best known of this style.

Extruders come with a selection of dies. Extruders marketed to home cooks typically include dies for spaghetti, bucatini, macaroni, rigatoni, and fusilli. Dies for commercial machines are typically sold a la carte. Dies for both commercial and home extruders can be made of either Teflon plastic or bronze. Bronze dies are prized for the rough texture they impart to the pasta, which gives sauce something to cling to. Teflon dies, on the other hand, minimize friction, making it possible to extrude pasta more quickly and with less force.

The pressure with which the dough is forced and the shape of the holes in the die determine the type of pasta that is formed. You can't necessarily tell by

looking at the front of a die what shape pasta it will make. Pasta may twist, wave, and curl as it comes out.

Once you get a feel for the dough, you will see that using an extruder is as easy as can be. In fact, I'd say that using an extruder is easier than using a sheeter or a cavatelli machine.

Pasta made with an extruder is firm with a satisfying chew.

EXTRUDER DIE SCIENCE IN A NUTSHELL

I find it endlessly amusing to watch how pasta emerges from a die, and viewers of my Noodlevision posts on Instagram seem to agree (page 201). For all of us who are fascinated and even mesmerized by this pasta dance, my resident science guy offers up an explanation of the science: non-Newtonian fluid flow. Non-Newtonian fluids such as pasta dough (and also ketchup, a better known example), flow with viscosity that varies depending on flow rates and shear forces applied. In other words, these substances can behave as either a liquid or a solid. This is why dough can twist, wave, and curl as it is extruded. Look at the back of different extruder dies to see how some are drilled to allow pasta dough to flow through certain areas faster than others.

THE CAVATELLI MAKER PASTA MACHINE

A cavatelli maker cuts and forms strips of dough into relatively small but thick pasta shells or dumplings. Using this type of pasta machine is an alternative to the time-consuming and skill-intensive task of making cavatelli, orecchiette, or gnocchetti one by one using a knife. Some cavatelli machines can make shells with different textures.

Most of the cavatelli makers on the market are freestanding machines. Some models attach to a pasta sheeter machine—the cavatelli attachment piggy-backs on the sheeter and shares the same crank arm. Otherwise, the sheeter functions as really nothing more than a base for stability.

Cavatelli, which is a relatively thick type of pasta, is generally hearty and has the most pronounced chewiness.

SHEETER VS. EXTRUDER VS. CAVATELLI MAKER PASTA MACHINE RECIPES

The key difference in making pasta dough for the sheeter, extruder, and cavatelli maker pasta machines is hydration, or water content. Recipes call for different amounts of water or eggs, which are largely water, yielding dryer and firmer dough or wetter and softer dough, depending on the type of pasta maker they are for.

HYDRATION PERCENTAGE

In pasta dough recipes, the weight of the water can be expressed as a percentage of the weight of the flour. The flour is always said to be 100%. So for example, if a recipe calls for 500 grams (1 lb. ⅔ ounces) of flour and 250 grams (8¾ ounces) of water, then we say it is 50% hydration.

Shelled eggs are about 75% water and yolks are about 50% water, so it is possible to estimate hydration percentages of pasta made with eggs or yolks.

The concept of hydration percentage makes it easier to understand and to compare different pasta recipes. It is also helpful for recipe formulation and for scaling recipes up and down, by which I mean multiplying and diving recipes to yield more or less servings.

PASTA SHAPES AND NAMES

· · · · ·

Pasta shapes made with the sheeter and cavatelli makers often have corresponding extruded shapes with the same or similar name. In most cases the resemblance is strong, other times you have to squint and use your imagination. To make matters more complicated, pasta shape names can vary according to the region of Italy. Sometimes the same shape can have different names and sometimes different shapes can have the same name. For example, they look alike at first glance, but sheeted garganelli is a ridged tube while extruded garganelli is a ridged twist. Thick spaghetti is known as bigoli in the Veneto region of Italy. Even I can hardly discern the difference between rigatoni and gargati and sedani. Just be aware as confusion can ensue!

WHY SO MANY PASTA SHAPES ANYWAY?

At this point you may be wondering why there are so many different types and shapes of pasta.

Availability of ingredients and tradition largely explain how different pastas came to be. Generally speaking, traditional pasta shapes from the north of Italy are made with soft flour and rich in eggs. Traditional pasta shapes from the south are made with semolina and water simply because those are the ingredients cooks had access to. Once pasta production was mechanized in factories, many extruded shapes meant to mimic traditional handmade shapes were developed.

Today, cooks are hardly limited by ingredient availability. We can choose a pasta shape based on mood, craving, and of course how it pairs with sauce. Certain shapes pair best with certain types of sauces. Silky sauces coat pasta strands and ribbons well. Chunky sauces partner nicely with chunky pastas. Cupped shapes act as scoops for sauce. Textured pastas, such as *rigate* or ridged shapes, have more surface area for sauce to cling to. All the variety keeps pasta endlessly interesting!

THE PASTA RAINBOW

· · · · ·

In addition to the many shapes, pasta can be made in a rainbow of colors using all-natural colorings. For instance, spinach can be used to make green pasta, and orange pasta can be made with tomato paste.

Colored pasta is usually all about visual interest and appeal. The taste of most of the colorings is quite mild and often unnoticeable.

PASTA-MAKING TOOLS AND EQUIPMENT

· · · · ·

In addition to your sheeter, extruder, and cavatelli maker, it's helpful to have the following cookware and utensils:

Scale: For measuring ingredients, particularly pasta dough ingredients. Cups and spoons, which are volume measures, are fine for measuring sauce ingredients. They are cumbersome and inaccurate for measuring flour. For example, the amount of flour in one single cup can vary by 28 grams (1 ounce) or more, depending on how densely it's packed. This error adds up quickly and it can lead to a very dry or sticky dough—and therefore much frustration. Weighing flour eliminates this problem altogether. It also happens to be quicker and easier, and it dirties less dishes. Weighing using metric units also has the added benefit of making it quite easy to do the math to scale recipes. This is true because, as you will soon learn, egg pasta doughs are simply 1 large egg per 100 grams (3½ ounces) of flour, and semolina pasta doughs made with water are formulated in terms of hydration percentage. Pasta dough recipes in this book were developed in grams; ounce measurements for pasta dough recipes are rounded. Pasta filling and sauce recipes were developed in cups, spoons, and ounces.

Large Broad, Shallow Bowl: For mixing pasta doughs by hand.

Food Processor: For mixing pasta doughs and making stuffed pasta fillings.

Stand Mixer: For mixing pasta doughs.

Blender: For making vegetable purées for colored pastas.

Work Surface: For mixing, kneading, forming, and laying out pasta. Pasta is least likely to stick to wood surfaces. Pasta may stick to smooth surfaces such as marble or stainless steel, so keep those surfaces dusted with flour or lay the pasta sheets on clean flour sack kitchen towels.

Bench Scraper: For mounding together dough ingredients, cutting pasta dough, and scraping work surfaces clean.

Straight Rolling Pin: For rolling out pasta dough.

Small and Large Pastry Brushes: For removing excess flour from pasta, applying water when making laminated pasta and sealing dumplings, and cleaning pasta machines.

Pasta or Noodle Knife: Straight-edged knife for cutting pasta sheets. The Japanese straight-edged knife design is known as a menkiri, soba kiri, or udon kiri.

Plain and Fluted Pastry Wheels: For cutting pasta sheets. Multi-wheel cutters are particularly useful, especially when making large quantities of uniform squares for filled pastas such as tortelloni, tortellini, and wontons.

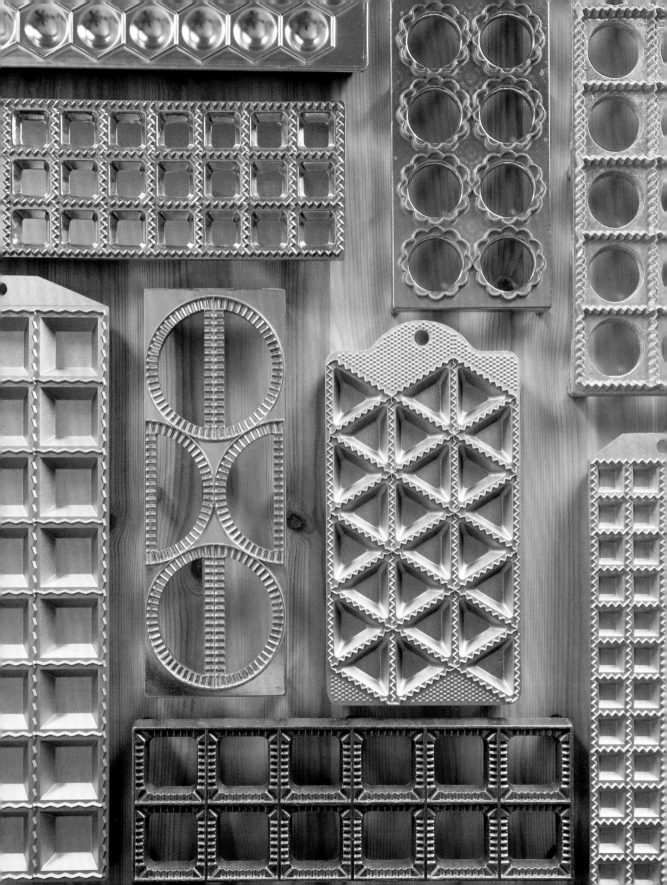

Plain and Fluted Round Cutter Sets: For cutting pasta sheets, especially when forming filled pastas such as ravioli, pelmeni, and pierogi.

Ravioli Stamps and Molds: For forming ravioli.

Spray Bottle: For misting pasta with water when sealing ravioli using a ravioli mold.

Fusilli Iron: A round, square, or hexagonal rod, now typically made of stainless steel or brass, for making fusilli. A bamboo skewer may be used if a fusilli iron is unavailable.

Cavarola: A carved or otherwise textured board, most often with a herringbone or scalloped pattern and typically made of wood, for embossing stracnar and other pasta shapes. Thickly sheeted pasta is rolled against the board using a rolling pin to emboss it.

Corzetti Stamp: A two-piece carved stamp with cutter, typically made of wood, for making corzetti. Thickly sheeted pasta is first cut into circles and then pressed between the two halves of the stamp to emboss it.

▲ Chitarra Cutter with Semolina and Oil Chitarra Pasta

Pettine or Garganelli Comb and Rolling Stick: A slatted or ridged board, typically made of wood, for making garganelli. Pasta squares are rolled around the rolling stick against the board to form ridges. A gnocchi board may be used if a pettine is unavailable.

Chitarra: A wooden frame strung with evenly spaced wires for making chitarra pasta. Thickly sheeted pasta is forced through the chitarra's wires using a rolling pin to cut it into individual strands.

Pasta Cutting Pins: Ridged rolling pins, typically made of wood or brass, for cutting pasta sheets into individual strands.

◄ Ravioli Stamps and Molds

Drying Rack or Screen: For laying out and drying pasta.

Flour Sack Towels: For lining work surfaces, pasta drying racks, and baking sheets to keep pasta from sticking. Also used for covering pasta for slow drying and for all manner of other cooking tasks.

Large Pot with Colander Insert(s): For boiling pasta. A pasta pot with colander insert is particularly useful for draining cooked pasta while reserving the pasta cooking water for adding to the sauce or for boiling another batch. Divided colander inserts make it especially quick and easy to plate individual noodle bowls and dishes such as ramen soup.

Colander: For draining cooked pasta.

Wire Skimmer: For gently removing cooked pasta and noodles from boiling water or hot oil. Particularly useful when cooking delicate dumplings.

Fine-Mesh Sieve: For straining and draining.

Fine Rasp-Style Grater: For fine grating of garlic, nutmeg, and hard cheese.

Large, Heavy Sauté Pan and Large, Heavy Pot or Dutch Oven: For making different types of pasta sauces.

Tongs: For tossing pasta with pasta sauce.

Straight Tweezer-Tongs: For flipping and manipulating small, delicate foods, tasting pasta to assess doneness, and using together with a ladle to form elegant pasta nests for serving.

Straight Carving Fork: For using together with a ladle to form elegant pasta nests for serving.

Ladle: For adding starchy pasta cooking water to the pasta sauce and for using together with tweezer-tongs to form elegant pasta nests for serving.

Heatproof Silicone Spoonula: Spoon/spatula hybrid for scraping up every last drop of sauce.

Candy/Jelly/Deep-Fry Thermometer: For monitoring fry oil temperature when deep frying.

Salt Pig: For having kosher salt at your fingertips for seasoning to taste.

Pepper Mill: For freshly ground black pepper for seasoning to taste.

Tasting Spoon: For tasting in order to make adjustments.

Pasta Fork or Pasta Tongs: For serving pasta.

Small Hand Broom and Dustpan: For sweeping dusting flour from the work surface.

And don't forget sharp knives, a honing steel, a generously sized cutting board, and bowls of all sizes for prepping food with safety and ease!

PASTA-MAKING INGREDIENTS

. . . . .

Always select the freshest and best quality ingredients possible; the dish will only be as good as the ingredients that go into it.

Flour

Wheat flour is the primary ingredient in pasta. It's what gives pasta its structure and texture. Different types of flour yield different results. In the United States, flour is classified by protein content.

Soft Wheat Flour: Relatively low in gluten-forming proteins.

Hard Wheat Flour: Relatively high in gluten-forming proteins.

All-Purpose Flour: The flour used most often in recipes in this book is unbleached all-purpose wheat flour. It is ground from the endosperm and has a creamy white color and a moderate protein content. AP flour yields a silky pasta with a lovely chew that is at once tender and resilient. I used King Arthur Flour AP flour, which has a consistent protein content of 11.7%, to develop these recipes. Do not use bleached flour, which is treated with bleaching agents for a whiter color, as it is too soft and also flavorless.

Semolina: Semolina is a coarse, golden flour ground from the endosperm of hard durum wheat. It is high in protein and yields chewy pasta. I used Bob's Red Mill semolina to develop recipes in this book.

GLUTEN

Gluten is formed when certain proteins in wheat flour are combined with water. Kneading, which is essentially a process of stretching and folding, develops gluten into an elastic network that allows pasta dough to hold together, giving it its elasticity and its chewy texture. Sheeting pasta continues the process of gluten development. Pasta doughs made from ingredients that are low in gluten tend to crumble and break.

Freshness of Flour—Flour is a staple pantry ingredient that's often taken for granted, but flour freshness matters. Store flour in an airtight container in a cool, dry place. Whole wheat flours have the shortest shelf life and are the most prone to going rancid. If you do not go through them relatively quickly consider storing them in the fridge or freezer.

ITALIAN FLOUR TERMINOLOGY

Farina: Flour. In Italy, flour is classified by type of wheat and grind.

Grano Tenero: Soft wheat.

Grano Duro: Hard, or durum, wheat.

Tipo 00: Also known as *doppio zero* or double zero, the finest grind of flour. (Tipo 0, Tipo 1, and Tipo 2 are progressively coarser.) This designation is independent of protein content and protein content varies from low to high.

Semola: Semolina.

Semola Rimacinata: A finer grind of semolina, double milled or *reground.* (Durum flour is finer still.) Feel free to experiment with substituting rimacinata for semolina in the recipes. It will yield pasta with slightly less coarse texture.

Integrale: Whole wheat.

Some cooks swear by Italian farina di grano tenero tipo 00 with a moderate protein content of about 12% that's formulated specifically for making pasta. One readily available brand is Caputo. In my experience, the difference between pasta made with 00 flour imported from Italy and pasta made with AP flour is not significant and it's not worth paying the premium for imported flour. But if you are a pasta-making fanatic, you may want to try it at least once and draw your own conclusions.

Sifting Flour—Generally it is not necessary to sift flour for making pasta. You can sift the flour if it seems to be particularly lumpy. You can also sift flour if you'd like to remove particles in order to refine it. For example, if you grind your own wheat you may choose to sift your whole wheat flour in order to remove bran.

Dusting Flour—When dusting pasta and work surfaces with flour to prevent sticking, I'll use AP flour if I'm making an AP flour pasta and I'll use semolina if I'm making a semolina pasta. I will say that semolina is great for this purpose because it's coarse and acts like little ball bearings—and later when it's time to cook the pasta, it does a great job of thickening and adding flavor to the sauce. Some cooks prefer rice flour for dusting because it absorbs moisture slowly. The point is it doesn't matter too much, just use whatever's handy.

Using room-temperature or slightly warm liquid ingredients will speed flour hydration.

If you'd like to bring eggs to room temperature in a hurry, place them in a bowl of warm (but not hot) water. Replace the water as it cools, until the eggs no longer feel cool to the touch. Dry the eggs before cracking them to avoid adding unwanted water.

Water

Water is just as important an ingredient in pasta as flour. Eggs, vegetable purées, and many other liquid ingredients contribute water to pasta recipes.

Eggs

Eggs are large grade AA. Eggs are approximately 75% water and so are one of the primary sources of hydration in pasta dough. Select farm fresh eggs with golden yolks for the best pasta.

Milk

Milk is whole cow's milk.

Cream

Cream is heavy cream. Opt for cream that is free of gums, thickeners, or stabilizers.

Butter

Butter is unsalted. Use real butter. Do not substitute margarine or other "buttery spreads."

Olive Oil

Olive oil is first cold pressed extra-virgin olive oil.

Balsamic Vinegar

Opt for balsamic vinegar that's imported from Italy and lists only wine vinegar and cooked grape must as ingredients. It should be relatively thick, almost syrupy, and have a complex sweet and sour flavor.

Wine

Pick out wine that's nice enough to drink with the meal.

Tomato Paste

Reach for paste in a tube when all you need is a couple of tablespoons.

Canned Whole Peeled Tomatoes

Choose D.O.P., or Denominazione d'Origine Protetta or Protected Designation of Origin, San Marzanos imported from Italy, which are made using tomatoes grown in the rich volcanic soil near Mount Vesuvius, for unparalleled sweetness and flavor.

Anchovies

Select anchovies packed in olive oil in glass jars.

Cheese

Parmigiano-Reggiano: The famous hard, granular cow's milk cheese is an indispensable ingredient in so many pasta dishes, adding salty umami flavor. Use real Parmigiano from Italy. Parmigiano is expensive, but a little bit goes a long way. If cost is a factor, try Grana Padano instead.

Pecorino Romano: This hard, granular sheep's milk cheese with a pungent, salty flavor is just as important as Parmigiano. Use real Pecorino from Italy.

Prosciutto

The famous dry-cured ham is another source of salt and umami in pasta dishes. Seek out either Prosciutto di Parma or Prosciutto di San Daniele imported from Italy.

Basil

Pick living basil, which is widely available now, for the most vibrant color and flavor. It never turns black and actually stays bright green even once cooked. Better yet, plant basil in your garden.

Red Chile Flakes

Known as *peperoncino* in Italian, this spice adds flavor as well as heat to pasta dishes. Add as much or as little to recipes as you see fit, depending on how spicy you like it.

Nutmeg

Buy whole nutmeg and grind it fresh using a rasp-style grater for the best flavor.

PREPARING HARD CHEESE

Buy Parmigiano, Pecorino, and other hard cheeses by the hunk and grate them yourself for the best, most intense flavor. To process, use a fine cheese grater or rasp-style grater. For large quantities, chunk it up and pulse it in a food processor. If you prefer large, ethereal shavings, use a vegetable peeler. Save rinds to throw into pots of ragu as they simmer.

Salt and Pepper

Salt adds flavor, and in pasta and noodle doughs its other primary function is increasing gluten strength. You may notice that salted dough seems to come together faster and benefits from longer resting times. Salt can also be added to keep noodles, particularly those containing acidic ingredients such as sourdough starter, from becoming too slippery once cooked.

Use kosher salt for its clean flavor and coarse grain. The size of the crystals makes kosher salt convenient to pinch and sprinkle, and it is visible on the surface of food, making it easier to gauge how much to use for seasoning. Kosher salt is inexpensive and available in supermarkets. I recommend Diamond Crystal kosher salt.

Flakey sea salt, such as fleur de sel or Maldon, can be used as a finishing salt when a little crunch and zing is desired.

Do not use iodized salt, which has a harsh metallic flavor.

Ground pepper loses its flavor and potency quickly. Keep black peppercorns in a mill and grind them as needed.

WHAT DOES "SEASON TO TASTE" MEAN?

Aside from recipes for pasta doughs, which call for salt by weight or in teaspoons when fractions of an ounce would be too small to be meaningful, most recipes don't prescribe quantities of salt to allow for variation in ingredients, differences in cooking (and especially reduction), and also personal taste.

So how do you determine how much salt to add? Salt is added to food to bring out its inherent flavors and make it taste better, not to make it taste salty. Food that doesn't have enough salt tastes flat and uninteresting, so it's important to know how to season correctly. Add a little salt at a time, and always taste as you go. When the flavors pop, and you can taste each individual component, the dish is seasoned perfectly. If you are unsure, simply remove a small amount of the food to a separate bowl and season it. Once you think it's perfect, add a little more salt and taste again. Does it taste better now, or is it just too salty? Now you have trained your palate, and you know exactly how the food should taste. Return this small amount to the rest of the food and season the entire quantity. Keep in mind that you can always add more salt to a dish, but you cannot take it out once you've added too much.

Adding pepper to taste isn't so technical; it's even more a matter of personal preference. So just go ahead and add as little or as much as you'd like.

WHAT IS A GENEROUS PINCH?

To give you a point of reference, my 3 to 4 finger "generous pinch" of kosher salt measures in at somewhere between a heaping ¼ teaspoon and ½ teaspoon. My "generous pinch" of spices such as nutmeg or cayenne is about ⅛ teaspoon.

HOW TO USE THIS BOOK

· · · · · ·

This is like a choose your own adventure book . . .

1. Pick a pasta machine. Do you want to use your sheeter? Do you have an extruder? Do you feel like making cavatelli? Then skip directly to that chapter.

2. Pick a pasta dough for that machine.

3. Pick a pasta shape. If it's a stuffed shape, pick a filling.

4. Pick a sauce. I make recommendations for pasta shapes and sauces, but feel free to mix and match as you like.

5. Cook, eat, and repeat!

PORTION SIZE

· · · · · ·

Figure 100 grams (3½ ounces) of flour and 1 egg yields one generous main-course serving. I believe most Italian cooks agree that it's "one egg of pasta" per person.

For pasta recipes made with water and little or no egg, figure 125 grams (4½ ounces) of flour yields one generous main-course serving.

A NOTE ON AUTHENTICITY

· · · · · ·

Many of these recipes are based on Italian culinary traditions, some on Chinese, Japanese, and others. While they are certainly inspired by these rich cuisines, I do not claim that they are authentic. I only claim that these recipes are delicious!

CHAPTER 1

Using the Sheeter Pasta Machine

DOUGH RECIPES FOR THE SHEETER

· · · · ·

BASIC SHEETER DOUGH FORMULATION

Use 1 large egg per 100 grams (3½ ounces) of unbleached all-purpose flour.

Use 50 grams (1¾ ounces) of water per 100 grams (3½ ounces) of unbleached all-purpose flour, or 50% hydration.

Egg Pasta

YIELDS 4 MAIN-COURSE SERVINGS

This is the quintessential pasta recipe, the sort that's common in the north of Italy. It yields a silky, rich pasta with a tender yet slightly chewy texture. The ratio to remember is 1 large egg to 100 grams (3½ ounces) of flour. "One egg of pasta" yields one generous serving.

400 g (14 oz) unbleached all-purpose flour

4 eggs, preferably at room temperature

To mix the dough and prepare it for the machine, see page 40.

Tomato Variation: Use tomato paste for a hint of sweetness and a pale orange color. Blend 30 grams (1 ounce) of tomato paste with the eggs before mixing the dough.

Porcini Variation: Use porcini mushrooms for a speckled light brown pasta with a subtle earthy aroma and flavor. Grind dried porcini mushrooms in a spice mill until powdered and sift through a fine-mesh sieve. Grind and sift any coarse bits again until they pass through the sieve. Blend 7 grams (¼ ounce) porcini powder with the flour before mixing the dough. Feel free to double or even triple the amount of porcini powder if you want a more pronounced flavor, but the dough might require an extra few drops of water.

Squid Ink Variation: Squid ink, which is available in tiny packets at fishmongers and gourmet grocers, makes for jet-black pasta with a hint of briny flavor. It's perfect with seafood sauces. Blend 7 grams (¼ ounce) of squid ink with the eggs before mixing the dough. Squid ink doesn't seem to want to dissolve easily, so start by loosening it up with just a spoonful of egg white before mixing it with the remaining quantity of egg.

Egg Fettucine ▶

All Yolk Pasta

Pasta made with only egg yolks is exquisite. It is rich and flavorful, and it has a wonderful snappy texture that's less chewy than pasta made with whole eggs. Of course, it's relatively expensive as it requires a dozen and a half eggs or more for just four dinner-size portions, but it's an excellent choice for when you want to indulge.

You can expect all yolk dough to be more challenging to bring together and more challenging to knead. This is because egg yolks are relatively low in moisture and the fat they contain shortens the gluten.

405 g (14¼ oz) unbleached all-purpose flour

325 g (11½ oz) (18 to 20) egg yolks, preferably at room temperature

To mix the dough and prepare it for the machine, see page 40.

Spinach Egg Pasta

This recipe yields a vibrant green dough with a hint of spinach flavor. The same technique can be used with chard, kale, arugula, pea shoots, radish tops, nettles, ramps, basil, parsley, or virtually any other greens; however, greens that are less likely to oxidize are not necessarily cooked before blending.

Kosher salt

85 g (3 oz) baby spinach

4 eggs, preferably at room temperature

410 g (14½ oz) unbleached all-purpose flour

Bring a large pot of water to a boil and salt generously. Add the spinach and boil until wilted, about 30 seconds. Drain the spinach and transfer to a large bowl of ice water to cool as quickly as possible. Drain the spinach again and squeeze out as much water as possible.

Combine the spinach and eggs in a blender and blend until smooth before mixing the dough. To mix the dough and prepare it for the machine, see page 40.

Chive Egg Pasta

Herbs are often blended using the same technique as for Spinach Egg Pasta (at left) before being added to pasta dough but they can also be minced for a speckled effect.

Olive oil in the dough is for an extra bit of richness and tenderness.

400 g (14 oz) unbleached all-purpose flour

4 eggs, preferably at room temperature

12 g (¼ cup) minced chives

15 g (½ oz) extra-virgin olive oil

To mix the dough and prepare it for the machine, see page 40.

◄ Spinach Egg Pasta

Beet Egg Pasta

YIELDS 4 MAIN-COURSE SERVINGS

Make this recipe when you want a bright fuchsia dough with a noticeably earthy flavor.

1 small (about 70 g [2½ oz]) beet

4 eggs, preferably at room temperature

440 g (15½ oz) unbleached all-purpose flour

Preheat the oven to 400°F (200°C, or gas mark 6).

Wrap the beet in foil and bake until tender to the center when tested with a paring knife, about 45 minutes. Let cool to room temperature and peel.

Combine 50 grams (1¾ ounces) of the beet and the eggs in a blender. Blend until smooth and strain through a fine-mesh sieve, if desired, before mixing the dough. To mix the dough and prepare it for the machine, see page 40.

Corn Egg Pasta

YIELDS 4 MAIN-COURSE SERVINGS

This is a bright yellow pasta with the aroma and sweetness of corn. It is delicate and slightly prone to breakage due to the cornmeal, so sheet the dough relatively thick and cut medium-length tagliatelle or wider pasta.

Kernels from 1 large ear corn

55 g (2 oz) water, preferably lukewarm

420 g (14¾ oz) unbleached all-purpose flour

80 g (2¾ oz) fine cornmeal

3 eggs, preferably at room temperature

Combine the corn kernels and water in a blender, blend until smooth, and force through a fine-mesh sieve to remove the skins. Use 135 grams (4¾ ounces) of the corn purée to mix the dough. To mix the dough and prepare it for the machine, see page 40.

Sweet Potato Egg Pasta

YIELDS 4 MAIN-COURSE SERVINGS

This pasta dough is a pretty pale orange with a hint of sweetness.

1 small (about 120 g [4¼ oz]) garnet yam

4 eggs, preferably at room temperature

445 g (15⅔ oz) unbleached all-purpose flour

Preheat the oven to 400°F (200°C, or gas mark 6).

Bake the yam on a rack on a baking sheet until tender to the center when tested with a paring knife, about 45 minutes. Let cool to room temperature and peel.

Combine 70 grams (2½ ounces) of the yam and the eggs in a blender. Blend until smooth before mixing the dough. To mix the dough and prepare it for the machine, see page 40.

Chocolate Egg Pasta

YIELDS 4 MAIN-COURSE SERVINGS

Pasta made with a small amount of cocoa powder has an unmistakable chocolate aroma and hint of bitterness. The striking deep brown color and complex flavor are lovely with savory as well as sweet sauces.

370 g (13 oz) unbleached all-purpose flour

30 g (1 oz) cocoa powder, sifted

4 eggs, preferably at room temperature

15 g (½ oz) water, preferably lukewarm

To mix the dough and prepare it for the machine, see page 40.

Milk Pasta, Green Tea Noodles, Tomato Egg Pasta, Semolina and Oil Pasta, Chocolate Egg Pasta ▶

Half Whole-Wheat Egg Pasta

YIELDS 4 MAIN-COURSE SERVINGS

A blend of equal parts whole wheat and all-purpose flour yields a brown-colored pasta with a wheaty flavor and silky texture. Whole wheat flour is more thirsty than all-purpose flour, so a tiny bit of water is required in addition to the eggs.

200 g (7 oz) unbleached all-purpose flour

200 g (7 oz) whole wheat flour

4 eggs, preferably at room temperature

15 g (½ oz) water, preferably lukewarm

To mix the dough and prepare it for the machine, see page 40.

Rye Egg Pasta

YIELDS 4 MAIN-COURSE SERVINGS

This is a dark pasta with a hearty bite and deep earthy flavor. The dough will feel crumbly at first, but it will come together with vigorous mixing.

270 g (9½ oz) unbleached all-purpose flour

135 g (4¾ oz) dark rye flour

4 eggs, preferably at room temperature

10 g (⅓ oz) water, preferably lukewarm

To mix the dough and prepare it for the machine, see page 40.

Chestnut Egg Pasta

YIELDS 4 MAIN-COURSE SERVINGS

Silky chestnut flour, which is available from some gourmet grocers and online, gives this pasta a creamy brown color and a sweet and slightly smoky flavor. Serve it with Sage Brown Butter (page 110) and sautéed wild mushrooms, chanterelles or porcinis would be particularly delicious. Or toss it with Gorgonzola dolce, walnuts, and sautéed pears. Or go all out and make tortelloni with a mixture of Ricotta Filling (page 62) and puréed roasted chestnuts.

280 g (9⅞ oz) unbleached all-purpose flour

120 g (4¼ oz) chestnut flour, sifted

4 eggs, preferably at room temperature

To mix the dough and prepare it for the machine, see page 40.

Duck Egg Pasta

YIELDS 4 MAIN-COURSE SERVINGS

Duck eggs are a rare treat. If you can find them at the market, don't hesitate to buy them. They are rich and flavorful, and they make excellent pasta. Duck eggs are a bit larger than hen eggs, so a bit more flour is required.

410 g (14½ oz) unbleached all-purpose flour

4 duck eggs, preferably at room temperature

To mix the dough and prepare it for the machine, see page 40.

Semolina and Oil Pasta

YIELDS 4 MAIN-COURSE SERVINGS

This is as close as you can get to the texture and flavor of pasta made with an extruder or cavatelli maker using a sheeter. It's relatively firm and chewy, though the olive oil does contribute a touch of tenderness.

350 g (12⅓ oz) semolina

150 g (5⅓ oz) unbleached all-purpose flour

250 g (8¾ oz) water, preferably lukewarm

15 g (½ oz) extra-virgin olive oil

To mix the dough and prepare it for the machine, see page 40.

Saffron Semolina and Oil Pasta

YIELDS 4 MAIN-COURSE SERVINGS

This pasta is colored with saffron. It is especially delicious with seafood sauces.

250 g (8¾ oz) boiling water

Several generous pinches saffron

350 g (12⅓ oz) semolina

150 g (5⅓ oz) unbleached all-purpose flour

15 g (½ oz) extra-virgin olive oil

Pour the boiling water over the saffron and let cool until lukewarm before mixing the dough. To mix the dough and prepare it for the machine, see page 40.

Half Semolina Egg Pasta

YIELDS 4 MAIN-COURSE SERVINGS

A blend of equal parts semolina and all-purpose flour yields a firmer, chewier pasta.

200 g (7 oz) unbleached all-purpose flour

200 g (7 oz) semolina

4 eggs, preferably at room temperature

To mix the dough and prepare it for the machine, see page 40.

Milk Pasta

YIELDS 4 MAIN-COURSE SERVINGS

This is a snowy white pasta with a mild flavor that contains no egg.

500 g (1 lb. 1⅔ oz) unbleached all-purpose flour

250 g (8¾ oz) whole milk, preferably at room temperature

To mix the dough and prepare it for the machine, see page 40.

All-Purpose Noodles

YIELDS 4 MAIN-COURSE SERVINGS

This dough is a great choice for all manner of dumplings, such as wontons, pelmeni, and pierogi. It can also be used for noodles for soups, stir-fries, and noodle bowls.

500 g (1 lb. 1⅔ oz) unbleached all-purpose flour

2 g (½ teaspoon) kosher salt

200 g (7 oz) water, preferably lukewarm

1 egg, preferably at room temperature

15 g (½ oz) canola oil

To mix the dough and prepare it for the machine, see page 40.

Sourdough Noodles

YIELDS 4 MAIN-COURSE SERVINGS

If you make sourdough, then no doubt you have a lot of excess starter after every feeding. You probably already know to use it in baked goods such as pancakes and waffles, but did you know that extra starter can also be used to make noodles?

This recipe is formulated using a liquid levain-type sourdough starter that's 125% hydration. If your starter differs from that, adjust the flour or water accordingly to obtain a firm dough that's not at all sticky. The acidity of the starter makes for an extensible dough that develops very quickly.

Of course this dough will ferment and rise during the resting time, so when you wrap it in plastic wrap to keep it from drying out, leave some room for expansion. The normal 1- to 2-hour dough resting time will result in noodles that have only a hint of sourdough aroma and flavor. For a more pronounced flavor, increase the resting time to 5 hours or more, or, to borrow a bread baker's term, retard overnight in the refrigerator.

Sheet this dough relatively thick and cut the noodles ¼ inch (6 mm) or wider. Do not allow these noodles to dry. I recommend cooking them immediately after sheeting.

375 g (13¼ oz) unbleached all-purpose flour

1½ g (scant ½ teaspoon) kosher salt

60 g (2 oz) sourdough starter

120 g (4¼ oz) water, preferably lukewarm

1 egg, preferably at room temperature

To mix the dough and prepare it for the machine, see page 40.

Whey Noodles

YIELDS 4 MAIN-COURSE SERVINGS

The acidity of whey creates a very extensible dough that makes delicious slippery noodles. I recommend cutting these short and wide, which is most easily achieved by slicing the sheeted dough crosswise into 1-inch (2.5-cm) strips.

500 g (1 lb. 1⅔ oz) unbleached all-purpose flour

250 g (8¾ oz) whey (page 191), preferably at room temperature

To mix the dough and prepare it for the machine, see page 40.

Green Tea Noodles

YIELDS 4 MAIN-COURSE SERVINGS

This dough is a deep green with a hint of bitter, vegetal tea flavor. I like to sheet it relatively thick and then cut it into wide noodles that are perfect for slurping in Asian-style noodle bowls and stir-fries. It could also be used for wontons and other Asian-style dumplings.

480 g (1 lb. 1 oz) unbleached all-purpose flour

20 g (¾ oz) matcha, sifted

2 g (½ teaspoon) kosher salt

250 g (8¾ oz) water, preferably lukewarm

15 g (½ oz) canola oil

To mix the dough and prepare it for the machine, see page 40.

Udon

YIELDS 4 MAIN-COURSE SERVINGS

Udon is a thick, chewy wheat noodle from Japan. It is almost snowy white and has an extremely bouncy and springy texture. Udon is served in noodle soup, stir-fries, or cold with a dipping sauce.

The relatively high salt content of this noodle increases gluten strength significantly, so the dough is quite tough. It is so tough, in fact, that it is not uncommon for udon dough to be kneaded by foot. Try it if you like: simply place the dough into a large zip-top bag, and walk on it (wearing a clean pair of socks, please!), folding it periodically, until it's smooth and elastic.

Be sure to rest the dough thoroughly before sheeting. Cut the dough into quarters rather than eighths. If the gluten isn't fully developed, it's likely to tear and shred when you begin, so fold the dough over and sheet it at the widest setting again and again, perhaps 5 or 6 times, until it smooths out. Once the dough is smooth you're probably done sheeting—dough sheets for udon noodles should be about ⅛ inch (3 mm) thick, so the widest setting of the rollers is likely just right (at least it is on my KitchenAid sheeter attachment). Cut the sheets into about ⅛-inch (3-mm)-wide noodles. Because they are so thick, it's not a good idea to let udon dry.

500 g (1 lb. 1⅔ oz) unbleached all-purpose flour

10 g (⅓ oz) kosher salt

210 g (7½ oz) water, preferably lukewarm

To mix the dough and prepare it for the machine, see page 40.

Ramen

YIELDS 4 MAIN-COURSE SERVINGS

Ramen is the popular Japanese alkaline noodle that's most often slurped in a rich and flavorful broth. It can be topped with any number of garnishes, but pork belly, soft-cooked eggs, and nori are favorites.

Typically yellow in color, ramen has an earthy aroma, a slippery texture, and firm, springy chew. It gets its color and mouthfeel from kansui, the clear liquid which is also known as potassium carbonate and sodium bicarbonate solution or simply lye water. Look for kansui at Asian markets or online, and feel free to experiment with the amount you use in your ramen within the range I've recommended below. Just 7 grams (¼ ounces) makes quite a noticeable difference in the boldness of the color and flavor, so tailor your noodles to suit your own taste.

Ramen dough is quite tough and shaggy, so don't expect to knead it by hand until it is smooth. Instead, let the pasta machine do much of the work of developing the gluten. Be sure to rest the dough thoroughly before sheeting. It's likely to tear and shred when you begin sheeting, so fold the dough over and sheet it at the widest setting again and again, perhaps 5 or 6 times, until it smooths out before narrowing the rollers and continuing. Sheet the dough relatively thick.

500 g (1 lb. 1⅔ oz) unbleached all-purpose flour

215 g (7½ oz) water, preferably lukewarm

21 to 28 g (¾ to 1 oz) kansui

To mix the dough and prepare it for the machine, see page 40.

Soba

YIELDS 4 MAIN-COURSE SERVINGS

Soba is a Japanese buckwheat noodle most often served cold with a dipping sauce.

Traditionally soba is made with either 100% buckwheat flour or 80% buckwheat flour and 20% wheat flour. Since buckwheat has no gluten, 100% buckwheat soba is extremely difficult to make and even 80% buckwheat soba requires great skill. I have increased the proportion of wheat flour to 30% in order to give a bit more margin for error, but I would still consider this a challenging recipe. Try it once you feel confident with your pasta-making skills.

Select a light, finely ground buckwheat flour for making soba. Whole-grain or dark buckwheat flour with black specks, which includes the hulls of the grain, will make for a dough that's far too crumbly.

This dough is fairly easy to mix, but the challenge comes when sheeting and cutting the noodles. The dough dries out quickly and becomes crumbly and prone to breakage, so work with a sense of urgency and keep pieces of dough as well as sheets and noodles covered with flour sack towels or plastic wrap throughout the process. Proceed immediately from sheeting to cutting to cooking the noodles, and do not allow any drying time between steps. It is a good idea to bring the pot of water to a boil while you are making the noodles. Also, cut each sheet in half for shorter noodles that are easier to handle. The sheets should be relatively thick—I stop at setting number 2 on my KitchenAid sheeter attachment—and cut into square noodles.

350 g (12⅓ oz) refined buckwheat flour

150 g (5⅓ oz) unbleached all-purpose flour

250 g (8¾ oz) water, preferably lukewarm

To mix the dough and prepare it for the machine, see page 40.

Gluten-Free Chickpea Pasta

YIELDS 4 MAIN-COURSE SERVINGS

Making gluten-free pasta is quite different from making wheat flour pasta. Gluten-free dough is extremely crumbly because of the lack of elasticity. But here's a dough for the sheeter that actually works, and the ingredient list for the recipe is short and sweet. Everything that's required is recognizable and easy to find, and it doesn't contain any gums or stabilizers.

There is no need to knead this dough. Just mix it until no dry ingredients remain. Wrap it and give it about 15 minutes of resting time to allow the chickpea flour to hydrate. Sheet only 3 or 4 portions of the dough at time, keeping the remaining dough covered to prevent it from drying out. Flatten each portion of dough with the heel of your hand and then even it out using a rolling pin until it is only slightly thicker than the widest setting on the pasta machine before sheeting; otherwise, it will just shred. There's also no need to fold the dough and pass it through the widest setting more than once, but if it does fall apart it can be patched together again. Dusting isn't necessary as it hardly sticks. The sheets should be left relatively thick—I do not sheet past setting number 3 on my KitchenAid sheeter attachment—and cut no narrower than fettuccine.

During cooking this pasta will foam up, so watch that it doesn't boil over.

4 eggs, preferably at room temperature

20 g (¾ oz) extra-virgin olive oil

440 g (15½ oz) chickpea flour

Blend the eggs and olive oil before mixing the dough. To mix the dough and prepare it for the machine, see page 40.

INSTRUCTIONS FOR THE SHEETER

· · · · ·

MIXING AND KNEADING DOUGH FOR THE SHEETER BY HAND

Mixing pasta dough by hand for the sheeter is quite easy and straightforward. Blend the dry ingredients, add the wet ingredients, and mix until a rough dough forms. Some cooks prefer to do this in the Italian style directly on a wooden board, making a mound of flour with a well in the center, adding the wet ingredients into the well, and then bringing the dough together using a fork. Other cooks prefer to mix the dough in a large, broad bowl using just their hands. Cooks using the well method stir the flour into the eggs gradually, while others mix the eggs all through the flour from the get-go.

Mixing by hand is my own preferred method of making dough for the sheeter because it's easy and generates the least dirty dishes. I usually mix in a bowl with just my hands, though sometimes I do it using a pair of cooking chopsticks. I like to mix the wet ingredients all through the dry ingredients, distributing them as evenly as possible. This creates lots of small shaggy bits that I then squeeze and press firmly together and into any loose dry ingredients at the bottom of the bowl to pick them up. I suggest you experiment with the different approaches and decide which is most comfortable for you.

The amount of flour needed may vary slightly depending on the brand of the flour, the size of the eggs, and the humidity. Keep in mind that it's much easier to add flour to a wet dough than it is to add liquid to a dry dough, so you can hold back a bit of the flour at first and then add more if the dough feels sticky. However, if it is a dry day and the dough simply won't come together, just add a little splash of water. You're after a tough, firm dough that isn't at all sticky. Soft doughs are prone to sticking and will not hold their shape when formed.

If you've mixed your dough in a bowl, transfer it to a wooden work surface now.

Knead the dough until it is smooth and elastic, about 10 minutes. Kneading will be a little bit of a workout. If you or the dough need a break, by which I mean the dough feels resistant to kneading or seems to be tearing, wrap the dough in plastic wrap or cover with an inverted bowl and let rest for a few minutes. Kneading should be much easier once you come back to it. The dough is ready when it springs back readily when poked. If there are any dry bits of dough on the kneading surface, take care to avoid working them into the dough.

Wrap the dough tightly in plastic wrap to keep it from drying out.

THE ULTIMATE PASTA MACHINE COOKBOOK

USING A FOOD PROCESSOR TO MIX DOUGH FOR THE SHEETER

Blend the dry ingredients in a food processor. Add the wet ingredients and process until all of the dry ingredients are moistened and a lumpy dough forms, about 30 seconds. Transfer the dough to a work surface, knead a moment or two until smooth, and wrap tightly in plastic wrap to keep it from drying out.

Dough made in a food processor is done in the blink of an eye, but washing the blade and work bowl, in my opinion, takes more time and effort than it's worth.

USING A STAND MIXER TO MIX DOUGH FOR THE SHEETER

Blend the dry ingredients in a mixer fitted with a paddle attachment. Blend together all of the wet ingredients. With the motor running on low speed, slowly trickle in the wet ingredients a tiny bit at a time until completely absorbed and a lumpy dough forms. Transfer the dough to a work surface, knead a moment or two until smooth, and wrap tightly in plastic wrap to keep it from drying out.

Firm pasta dough can strain the stand mixer motor or cause the mixer bowl to pop off. Exercise care.

RESTING THE DOUGH FOR THE SHEETER

Let the dough rest at room temperature for at least an hour and preferably two. The resting time allows the flour to fully hydrate and gives the gluten a chance to relax so that the dough rolls out easily without tearing.

MAKING DOUGH FOR THE SHEETER IN ADVANCE

At this point you can refrigerate the wrapped pasta dough for up to 24 hours. I don't recommend keeping pasta dough containing egg longer than a day because quality degrades. The discoloration due to oxidation becomes too unappetizing. Bring refrigerated pasta dough to room temperature before sheeting.

DOUGH WORKING TEMPERATURE

Cold dough is hard, and warm dough is soft and sticky. Room temperature dough is ideal to work with.

CUTTING EQUAL PIECES OF DOUGH WITHOUT GETTING OUT YOUR SCALE

Cut the ball of dough in half. Cut each half into half again, and then cut each quarter into half again.

SHEETING THE PASTA WITH THE MACHINE

Sheeting pasta requires quite a bit of counter space, so clear the decks. Work quickly to prevent the pasta from drying out. Cut the dough into eighths. Flatten one portion of dough into a strip and, starting with the narrow end, pass it through a pasta machine with the rollers at the widest setting. Fold the pasta neatly in thirds and pass it through the machine again, this time with the folds perpendicular to the rollers. Pass the remaining portions of dough through the pasta machine in the same manner.

If there's any tearing, repeat folding the pasta in thirds and sheeting it at the widest setting until it smooths out before continuing. At this point, if any of the sheets aren't quite rectangular, you can give them a gentle tug to encourage them into shape. Close the rollers down one notch and pass each pasta sheet through the pasta machine once. Continue passing the pasta sheets through the pasta machine with the rollers at successively narrower settings until the pasta sheets are the desired thickness. The pasta will get longer and longer as it gets thinner.

For most shapes, pasta is rolled until translucent, perhaps the second-to-last or third-to-last narrowest setting of the rollers (settings differ on each brand of machine), but thickness is largely a matter of personal preference. Go thicker if you are making a stamped or embossed pasta or prefer a substantial noodle, thinner if you prefer it to be more delicate.

I use setting number 5 on my KitchenAid sheeter attachment most often, especially for ribbon-shaped pasta. For *relatively thick* sheets I use setting number 4 unless otherwise indicated, for *relatively thin* sheets I use setting number 6.

RELATIVE THICKNESS OF PASTA SHAPES

Thickness settings differ on each brand of sheeter, and settings are marked with numbers and not actual thickness measurements. The following chart of the settings I use on my KitchenAid gives a sense of relative thickness.

SELECTED PASTA/ NOODLE SHAPES FROM THICKEST TO THINNEST	SUGGESTED KITCHENAID SHEETER ATTACHMENT SETTING
Udon	1
Soba	2
Spaghetti, Spaghetti Quadri, and Chitarra	2 or 3
Gluten-Free Chickpea Pasta Shapes	3
Ramen	3 or 4
Noodles	4
Corzetti	4
Crackers	4
Cannoli	4
Pelmeni and Pierogi	4 or 5
Lasagna	5
Pappardelle, Tagliatelle, Fettuccine, and Tagliolini	5 or 6
Farfalle and Garganelli	5 or 6
Ravioli	5 or 6
Tortelloni, Tortellini, and Agnolotti	6

Dust the pasta sheets lightly with flour if there's any sign of sticking while sheeting. As you work, lay the pasta sheets flat in a single layer on a wooden surface or flour sack towels. Handle them gently to avoid stretching and tearing, draping them over the backs of your hands rather than holding them with your fingertips.

This method is efficient and results in relatively consistent rectangular sheets of pasta that are the width of the pasta machine and a manageable length. If the pasta sheets turn out a bit narrow, don't worry about it and try to make them wider next time. If the pasta sheets get too long to work with comfortably, feel free to cut them into shorter lengths.

When using stand mixer sheeter and cutter attachments, run the stand mixer on low to medium-low speed.

When you're done sheeting, you can trim the ends of the pasta sheets to create neat rectangles. But it's not absolutely necessary if a little variance in the length of your noodles doesn't bother you.

LAMINATING PASTA

Sheeted pasta can be laminated in different ways for visually stunning effects. Any pasta shape can be made using laminated pasta, but it's especially lovely for creating ravioli and other dumplings, as well as shapes such as farfalle and garganelli.

Laminating Herbs and Flowers

Using either a bit of pressure or the lightest brushing of water as glue, sandwich tender herb leaves and/or the petals of edible flowers between two pieces of sheeted pasta. Open the pasta machine rollers up one notch and pass the pasta sheet through the pasta machine to laminate. Continue passing the laminated pasta sheet through the pasta machine with the rollers at successively narrower settings until the pasta sheet is translucent and the herbs and flowers are visible. The herbs and flowers will appear stretched out.

Parsley-Laminated Egg Pasta ▶

Laminating Colors

Using either a bit of pressure or the lightest brushing of water as glue, make a design using pieces of one or more colors of sheeted pasta cut into the desired shapes on a sheet of pasta of a different color. The design can be as simple as stripes or dots or as complex as a portrait. Open the pasta machine rollers up one notch and pass the pasta sheet through the pasta machine to laminate. Continue passing the laminated pasta sheet through the pasta machine with the rollers at successively narrower settings until the pasta sheet is the desired thickness. The original design will appear stretched out.

◀ Laminated Egg Pasta and Beet Egg Pasta

MARBLING COLORED PASTA

Lightly knead together two or more colors of pasta dough just until they adhere before sheeting. This will create pasta with a swirled, marbled effect. Making marbled pasta is a great way to use up scraps.

MAKING SHEETS OF PASTA IN ADVANCE

At this point you can refrigerate the sheeted pasta for up to 24 hours. To store, stack the pasta sheets between flour sack towels on a baking tray and wrap tightly in plastic wrap to keep it from drying out.

CUTTING AND FORMING THE PASTA SHEETS

Passing all of the pieces of pasta through each setting of the rollers is more efficient than sheeting one piece at a time, and it allows all of the sheets to dry at an even rate. However, hand-formed shapes such as garganelli, farfalle, ravioli, and tortellli must be made with freshly-rolled pasta that hasn't had much of a chance to dry and harden, so sheet and form just 1 or 2 pieces of dough at a time as you are comfortable. Alternatively, sheet all of the pasta, and stack sheets between flour sack towels to keep them from drying out.

For long-cut pasta such as fettuccine and spaghetti, allow sheets of pasta to dry a bit until they just start to feel leathery before cutting them. Strands of pasta cut from sheets that are too moist will stick to each other, and pasta sheets that are too dry will shatter when cut. Dust pasta sheets with flour if there's ever any sign of sticking, but try not to use any more flour than necessary; excess flour can be removed using a pastry brush. To cut sheeted pasta into ribbons or strands, dust it with flour and pass it through pasta machine cutters, discarding any narrow scraps from the edges, or fold it up loosely and slice it using a knife. For other shapes, use a straight or fluted pastry wheel or other specialized tool.

Try to make all of the pieces of pasta within each batch the same thickness and size, and pinch folds firmly so that they cook evenly.

PASTA VERSUS NOODLES

In my mind, all pastas are noodles but not all noodles are pasta. I use the term *noodle* to refer to any boiled sheeted and cut unleavened dough from anywhere in the world. But I call it *pasta* if it's a boiled sheeted and cut unleavened dough originating from Italy.

Egg Tagliatelle ▶

Cut and form the most common shapes
as follows:

Lasagna: Cut the sheeted pasta into 9-inch (23-cm)
lengths, or lengths the size of your baking dish, forming pasta sheets. Typically layered with filling and
sauce, and baked in the oven.

Cannelloni: Cut the sheeted pasta into 5-inch
(13-cm) squares, forming pasta sheets. Typically
rolled around a filling, covered in sauce, and baked
in the oven.

Fazzoletti: Cut the sheeted pasta into 3- to 4-inch
(7.5- to 10-cm) squares, forming pasta handkerchiefs.

Pappardelle: Cut the sheeted pasta into ½- to 1-inch
(1- to 2.5-cm)-wide strands, forming wide pasta ribbons. Usually shorter than narrower ribbon-shaped
pastas to make it easier to eat.

Reginette and Mafaldine: Cut the sheeted pasta into
¼- to ½-inch (6-mm to 1-cm)-wide strands using a
fluted cutter, forming pasta ribbons with wavy edges.

▲ Egg Lasagna

Corn Egg Reginette ▶

▲ Semolina and Oil Quadrucci

Tagliatelle: Cut the sheeted pasta into ¼- to ½-inch (6-mm to 1-cm)-wide strands, forming pasta ribbons.

Fettuccine: Cut the sheeted pasta into ¼-inch (6-mm)-wide strands, forming pasta ribbons.

Linguine: Cut the sheeted pasta into ⅛-inch (3-mm)-wide strands, forming narrow pasta ribbons.

Spaghetti Quadri and Soba: Cut thickly sheeted pasta into strands that are as wide as they are thick, forming square spaghetti.

Tagliolini: Cut the sheeted pasta into 1/16- to ³/32-inch (1- to 1.5-mm)-wide strands, forming very narrow pasta ribbons.

Angel Hair and Capellini: Cut the sheeted pasta into 1/32-inch (½-mm)-wide strands, forming extremely narrow pasta ribbons.

Quadrucci: Cut the sheeted pasta into ¼- to ½-inch (6-mm to 1-cm)-wide strands and then cut the strands crosswise, forming little pasta squares. Good for soup.

◀ Tomato Egg Fettuccine, Chocolate Egg Fettuccine,
 Milk Fettuccine, Green Tea Noodles

Farfalle: Cut the sheeted pasta into 1- to 1½-inch by 2-inch (2.5- to 3.5-cm by 5-cm) rectangles and pinch each rectangle firmly at the center, forming butterflies or bows.

Sorpresine: Cut the sheeted pasta into squares using a wheel cutter. To fold each dumpling, using a fingertip, lightly moisten two opposite corners of a pasta square with water—just the smallest amount of water will do. Bring the two moistened corners together and pinch firmly to seal, forming a triangle but without creasing the long side. Lightly moisten the corners of the pasta along the long side of the triangle with water. Bring the two corners together and pinch firmly to seal, forming unfilled hollow dumplings. Size varies. For when you are making tortelloni, tortelli, or tortellini and run out of filling.

Fusilli: Cut thickly sheeted pasta as for linguine or fettuccine and then roll each strand of pasta firmly at an angle around a fusilli iron or bamboo skewer, forming curled strands or ribbons, like ringlets or corkscrews. Best with Semolina and Oil Pasta (page 35).

Stracnar: Roll well-floured thickly sheeted pasta using a rolling pin against a cavarola to emboss it. Cut 1- by 2-inch (2.5- by 5-cm) pieces, forming embossed pasta rectangles.

▲ Semolina and Oil Fusilli

Half Whole-Wheat Egg Farfalle ▶

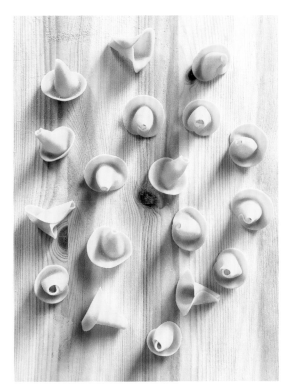

▲ Egg Cappellacci dei Briganti

Corzetti: Cut thickly sheeted pasta into circles using a corzetti cutter and press each well-floured circle between the two halves of a corzetti stamp, forming embossed pasta coins.

Garganelli: Cut the sheeted pasta into 1½- to 2-inch (3.5- to 5-cm) squares. Roll each pasta square, starting from a corner, around a rolling stick against a pettine or garganelli board, forming ridged tubes with pointed ends. A gnocchi board may be used if a pettine is unavailable.

Cappellacci dei Briganti: Cut the sheeted pasta into 1½- to 2-inch (3.5- to 5-cm) circles using a ravioli stamp or cookie cutter. Form each pasta circle into an open-ended cone with a brim, forming hat-shaped pasta.

Chitarra: Roll well-floured thickly sheeted pasta using a rolling pin against a chitarra to cut it, forming square spaghetti.

Noodles: Cut the sheeted dough into strands of the desired width, forming ribbons. This is a broad term and size varies.

SHEETED PASTA BLENDS

Paglia e Fieno: Blend equal amounts of Egg Tagliatelle (page 28 and 55) and Spinach Egg Tagliatelle (page 31 and 55) together, creating straw and hay–colored pasta.

◀ Porcini Egg Garganelli

STUFFED PASTA

· · · · ·

Prepare fillings, letting any cooked fillings cool to room temperature, before sheeting pasta.

In general, dough for Italian filled pastas such as ravioli, tortelloni, and tortellini should be sheeted relatively thin so that the filling and the pasta are cooked through at the same time. I usually use setting number 6 on my KitchenAid sheeter attachment, though on occasion I may use 5 for a more hearty ravioli. This is especially important for stuffed pasta with ricotta fillings as the ricotta could go grainy in the time it takes a thick noodle to cook through. Noodle dough for some hearty dumplings such as pierogi and pelmeni may be sheeted relatively thick, though some prefer more delicate thinner skins. I use settings 4 and 5 on the KitchenAid sheeter attachment.

Anything from ricotta to puréed vegetables to shredded meat can be stuffed inside of pasta, but fillings should not be too moist or they will soak through the pasta.

Ravioli of Chive Egg Pasta and Corn and Fresh Mozzarella Filling ▶

Ricotta Filling

YIELDS ENOUGH TO FILL APPROXIMATELY 1 RECIPE
FRESH EGG PASTA OR OTHER SHEETED PASTA,
MAKING 4 GENEROUS SERVINGS

This is a classic filling for ravioli and tortelloni.

Serve dumplings with Simple Tomato Sauce
(page 108) and top with plenty of Parmigiano.

1 lb. 2 oz (510 g) Homemade Ricotta (page 191)
or store-bought, at room temperature

1 oz (30 g) freshly grated Parmigiano-Reggiano

2 tablespoons (8 g) minced Italian parsley

1 clove garlic, grated using a rasp-style grater

Generous pinch freshly ground nutmeg

Kosher salt

Freshly ground black pepper

Blend together the ricotta, Parmigiano, parsley, garlic,
and nutmeg. Season with salt and pepper.

Spinach-Ricotta Filling

YIELDS ENOUGH TO FILL APPROXIMATELY 1 RECIPE
FRESH EGG PASTA OR OTHER SHEETED PASTA,
MAKING 4 GENEROUS SERVINGS

This is another classic filling for ravioli and tortelloni.

Serve ravioli with Sage Brown Butter (page 110),
and match tortelloni with Simple Tomato Sauce
(page 108) and top with plenty of Parmigiano.

Kosher salt

8 oz (225 g) baby spinach

1 lb. (455 g) Homemade Ricotta (page 191)
or store-bought, at room temperature

1 oz (30 g) freshly grated Parmigiano-Reggiano

1 clove garlic, grated using a rasp-style grater

Generous pinch freshly ground nutmeg

Freshly ground black pepper

Bring a large pot of water to a boil and salt generously.
Add the spinach and boil until wilted, about 30 seconds. Drain the spinach and transfer to a large bowl of
ice water to cool as quickly as possible. Drain the spinach again and squeeze out as much water as possible.
Mince coarsely.

Blend together the spinach, ricotta, Parmigiano, garlic,
and nutmeg. Season with salt and pepper.

Tortelloni of Spinach Egg Pasta and Spinach-Ricotta Filling ▶

Creamy Mushroom Filling

YIELDS ENOUGH TO FILL APPROXIMATELY 1 RECIPE FRESH EGG PASTA OR OTHER SHEETED PASTA, MAKING 4 GENEROUS SERVINGS

I like to use this filling to make agnolotti, but it would also be great for ravioli and tortelloni.

To serve, toss boiled dumplings with Homemade Cultured Butter (page 190) and top with grated Parmigiano, freshly ground black pepper, and a drizzle of real balsamic vinegar (pictured on page 106).

Substitute chanterelles for button mushrooms during their fall season and serve with Sage Brown Butter (page 110).

2 tablespoons (30 ml) extra-virgin olive oil

2 tablespoons (28 g) unsalted butter

10 oz (280 g) button or cremini mushrooms, sliced

1 clove garlic, minced

1 lb. (455 g) Homemade Ricotta (page 191) or store-bought, at room temperature

1 oz (30 g) freshly grated Parmigiano-Reggiano

Generous pinch freshly ground nutmeg

Kosher salt

Freshly ground black pepper

Heat a large, heavy skillet over medium heat until hot. Add the olive oil and butter and swirl to coat the inside of the pan. When the butter bubbles and the foam subsides, add the mushrooms. Sauté until tender and golden brown, about 8 minutes. Add the garlic and sauté until fragrant, about 30 seconds. Remove from the heat and let cool.

Combine the mushrooms, ricotta, Parmigiano, and nutmeg in a food processor. Process until smooth. Season with salt and pepper.

Corn and Fresh Mozzarella Filling

YIELDS ENOUGH TO FILL APPROXIMATELY 1 RECIPE FRESH EGG PASTA OR OTHER SHEETED PASTA, MAKING 4 GENEROUS SERVINGS

Take advantage of the summer corn season by making ravioli with this filling.

Serve corn ravioli topped with Basil Pesto (page 112) and possibly also Roasted Tomatoes (page 132).

Kosher salt

3 ears corn

8 oz (225 g) fresh mozzarella, diced and drained thoroughly on paper towels

3 oz (85 g) freshly grated Parmigiano-Reggiano

1 small clove garlic, minced

2 tablespoons (6 g) minced chives

Freshly ground black pepper

Bring a large pot of water to a boil and salt generously.

Add the corn to the boiling water and boil, stirring occasionally, until tender, about 10 minutes. Remove the corn to a plate using tongs and let cool to room temperature.

Blot the corn dry with paper towels. Cut the kernels off the ears.

Combine the corn kernels, mozzarella, Parmigiano, and garlic in a food processor. Process until smooth. Stir in the chives, and season with salt and pepper.

Classic Tortellini Filling

YIELDS ENOUGH TO FILL APPROXIMATELY 2 RECIPES
FRESH EGG PASTA OR OTHER SHEETED PASTA,
MAKING 8 GENEROUS SERVINGS

Tortellini are filled with a savory blend of browned pork and chicken, mortadella, prosciutto, Parmigiano, and nutmeg. Making tortellini in the traditional way is certainly a labor of love as each dumpling is hardly bigger than a thumbnail! But it is well worth the effort. Handmade tortellini are exquisite and perhaps the crown jewel of Bolognese cuisine.

It is unnecessary to add salt to this filling as the ingredients are already highly seasoned. When shaping these tortellini, there's really no need to moisten the edges of the pasta with water to seal as this filling does not ooze.

To cook tortellini, simmer them in Simple Chicken Stock (page 195) rather than just plain water. Serve them in the broth or drain and toss in cream that's been reduced until thick and seasoned with salt and pepper. Either way, top with plenty of grated Parmigiano.

Tortellini filling is a bit of a project, but it keeps well. So this recipe makes enough for a double batch of Egg Pasta. If you don't want to make that many tortellini in one go, simply freeze half of the filling for another time. Filling will keep for several weeks tightly sealed (preferably using a vacuum sealer) in the freezer.

1 tablespoon (15 ml) extra-virgin olive oil

1 tablespoon (14 g) unsalted butter, diced

7 oz (200 g) pork loin, cut into 1¼-inch (3-cm) pieces

7 oz (200 g) boneless skinless, chicken thighs, cut into 1¼-inch (3-cm) pieces

7 oz (200 g) mortadella, diced

2¾ oz (80 g) prosciutto, diced

2½ oz (70 g) freshly grated Parmigiano-Reggiano

Generous pinch freshly ground nutmeg

Freshly ground white pepper

1 egg

Heat a large, heavy skillet over medium heat until hot. Add the olive oil and butter and swirl to coat the inside of the pan. When the butter bubbles and the foam subsides, add the pork. Sauté until golden brown all over, about 4 minutes. Remove the pork to a plate using a slotted spoon. Add the chicken to the skillet. Sauté until golden brown all over and just cooked through, about 6 minutes. Remove the chicken to the plate using the slotted spoon. Let cool to room temperature.

Transfer the pork and chicken along with any accumulated juice to a food processor, add the mortadella, prosciutto, Parmigiano, nutmeg, and a generous grinding of white pepper. Process until a coarse purée. Add the egg and process until combined.

Butternut Squash Filling

YIELDS ENOUGH TO FILL APPROXIMATELY 1 RECIPE
FRESH EGG PASTA OR OTHER SHEETED PASTA,
MAKING 4 GENEROUS SERVINGS

Make ravioli or tortelloni with this filling in the fall when the winter squash harvest comes in.

Serve the squash dumplings with Sage Brown Butter (page 110) and plenty of grated Parmigiano.

1 medium (about 2 lb. 4 oz [1 kg]) butternut squash, halved and seeded

1 oz (30 g) freshly grated Parmigiano-Reggiano

Generous pinch freshly ground nutmeg

Kosher salt

Freshly ground black pepper

Preheat the oven to 400°F (200°C, or gas mark 6).

Bake the squash cut-side down on a baking sheet for 30 minutes. Flip the squash and bake until tender to the center when tested with a paring knife, about 45 minutes. Let cool.

When the squash is cool enough to handle, scoop the flesh out of the skin and purée it using a ricer or food mill. Let cool to room temperature.

Blend together 1 pound 3½ ounces (550 g) of the squash purée, Parmigiano, and nutmeg. Season with salt and pepper. Reserve the remaining squash purée for another use.

Pelmeni Filling

YIELDS ENOUGH TO FILL APPROXIMATELY 1 RECIPE
ALL-PURPOSE NOODLES, MAKING 4 TO 6 SERVINGS

Pelmeni are the comfort food of Russian cuisine, and I grew up on a steady diet of them. This is my mother's recipe for her delicious beef and pork filling. It's heavy on the onion and black pepper, which is why it's so good.

My mother makes large pelmeni. Each one is a great big mouthful. I make mine just a bit smaller, for a more dainty bite. I sheet my noodle dough to the same thickness as I sheet pasta, cut skins with a 2½-inch (6-cm) round cutter, and use a level teaspoon of filling for each dumpling.

Serve pelmeni topped with lots of black pepper and a generous dollop of sour cream.

Pelmeni are usually made in massive batches and stocked in the freezer. To freeze, arrange pelmeni in a single layer on parchment-lined baking sheets. Once they are solid, transfer the pelmeni to a zip-top bag. Pelmeni will keep for weeks tightly sealed in the freezer. Cook from frozen.

10⅔ oz (300 g) 20% fat ground beef

5⅓ oz (150 g) ground pork

1 yellow onion, grated

1 tablespoon (9 g) kosher salt

1 tablespoon (3 g) freshly ground black pepper

Blend together the ground beef, ground pork, onion, salt, and pepper.

Potato Pierogi Filling

YIELDS ENOUGH TO FILL APPROXIMATELY 1 RECIPE
ALL-PURPOSE NOODLES, MAKING 6 SERVINGS

Boiling potatoes whole so that they do not become waterlogged and then ricing instead of mashing them makes for a light and fluffy filling for the most delicate and delicious pierogi ever.

I sheet my noodle dough relatively thick as for noodles, cut skins with a 2¾-inch (7-cm) round cutter, and use a level tablespoon of filling for each dumpling.

Serve pierogi tossed with Homemade Cultured Butter (page 190).

Pierogi can be made in large batches and frozen. To freeze, arrange pierogi in a single layer on parchment-lined baking sheets. Once they are solid, transfer the pierogi to a zip-top bag. Pierogi will keep for weeks tightly sealed in the freezer. Cook from frozen.

2 large (about 2 lb. [920 g] in total) russet potatoes

Kosher salt

4 oz (110 g) unsalted butter, melted

2 tablespoons (30 g) sour cream

3 oz (85 g) shredded sharp Cheddar

3-4 green onions, sliced thinly

Freshly ground black pepper

Combine the potatoes and enough water to cover by several inches in a large, heavy pot. Bring to a boil, salt generously, and simmer until the potatoes are tender to the center when tested with a paring knife, about 50 minutes. Remove the potatoes from the boiling water and let cool.

When the potatoes are cool enough to handle, peel them and purée them using a ricer or food mill. Let cool to room temperature.

In a bowl, blend together the riced potatoes, butter, sour cream, Cheddar, and green onions. Season with salt and pepper.

Pork and Shrimp Wonton Filling

YIELDS ENOUGH TO FILL APPROXIMATELY ⅔ RECIPE
ALL-PURPOSE NOODLES, MAKING 4 TO 6 SERVINGS

This filling makes delicious wontons for soup (page 148) or for a fried appetizer (page 149). Or if you happen to have some Szechuan Chile Oil from making noodle bowls (page 144), simply boil them and serve them topped with the chile oil and cilantro, green onions, and a drizzle of soy sauce and Chinkiang vinegar.

Cut the noodle dough into 2½-inch (6-cm) squares and use a level teaspoon of filling for each dumpling.

Wontons can be made in large batches and frozen. To freeze, arrange wontons in a single layer on parchment-lined baking sheets. Once they are solid, transfer the wontons to a zip-top bag. Wontons will keep for weeks tightly sealed in the freezer. Cook from frozen.

12 oz (340 g) ground pork

4¾ oz (135 g) shrimp, peeled, deveined, and minced coarsely

1 green onion, sliced thinly

2 cloves garlic, minced

1 teaspoon ginger, minced

2 tablespoons (30 ml) soy sauce

¼ teaspoon toasted sesame oil

2 teaspoons (5 g) cornstarch

½ teaspoon sugar

Freshly ground white pepper

Blend together the ground pork, shrimp, green onion, garlic, ginger, soy sauce, sesame oil, cornstarch, sugar, and a generous grinding of white pepper.

FORMING STUFFED PASTA

When forming stuffed pasta, the ratio of pasta to filling is a personal preference. Some like dumplings that are all filling, others prefer dumplings with substantial pasta borders. Either way, it's a good idea to cut shapes as close together as possible to minimize scraps. Also keep in mind that, assuming the amount of filling per dumpling stays constant, the yield of dumplings will depend on how thin you sheet the pasta.

Cut and form the most common shapes as follows:

Ravioli and Anolini: Cut the sheeted pasta into pieces slightly longer than a ravioli mold. Dust a pasta sheet with flour on one side only. Lay it floured-side down on the ravioli mold. Place a small amount of filling into each depression. Using a spray bottle, lightly mist the pasta with water. Alternatively, use a fingertip or pastry brush dipped in water to moisten the edges of each raviolo—just the smallest amount of water will do. Drape another sheet of pasta over the filled mold, eliminating any air pockets as you go. Roll a rolling pin across the mold, pressing down hard to cut out the ravioli, forming flat dumplings. To remove the ravioli from the mold, invert it onto a lightly floured surface. If a ravioli mold is unavailable, sandwich evenly spaced bits of filling between sheets of pasta in the same manner, moistening the pasta around the filling with water and eliminating air pockets, and cut ravioli using a ravioli stamp, cookie cutter, or pastry wheel. Size and shape vary, though anolini are small and round.

Egg Yolk Ravioli: Using a piping bag fitted with a large plain tip, pipe circles of Ricotta Filling or Spinach-Ricotta Filling (page 62) that are just large enough to cradle an egg yolk on a sheet of pasta. Gently slip one yolk into each ricotta nest. Use a fingertip or pastry brush dipped in water to moisten the edges of each raviolo—just the smallest amount of water will do. Drape another sheet of pasta over the filling, and eliminating any air pockets as you go, firmly press the edges together to seal. Cut ravioli using a large plain or fluted round cutter, forming large, flat dumplings.

Triangoli: Cut the sheeted pasta into squares using a wheel cutter. Place a small amount of filling in the center of each pasta square. To fold each dumpling, using a fingertip, lightly moisten the edges of a pasta square with water—just the smallest amount of water will do. Fold the pasta in half over the filling, and eliminating any air pockets, firmly pinch the edges together to seal, forming triangle-shaped dumplings. Size varies.

Ravioli of Egg Pasta and Corn and Fresh Mozzarella Filling ▶

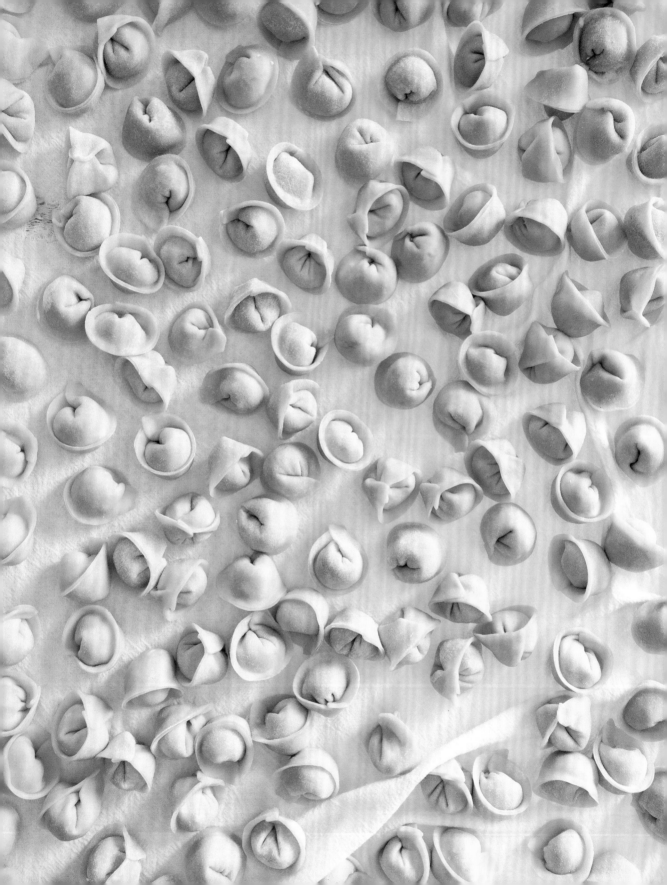

Mezzelune and Pierogi: Cut the sheeted pasta into circles using a ravioli stamp or cookie cutter. Place a small amount of filling in the center of each pasta circle. To fold each dumpling, using a fingertip, lightly moisten the edges of a pasta circle with water— just the smallest amount of water will do. Fold the pasta in half over the filling, and eliminating any air pockets, firmly pinch the edges together to seal, forming half-circle or half-moon-shaped dumplings. Size varies.

Pelmeni: Cut the sheeted pasta into circles using a plain round cutter or ravioli stamp. Place a small amount of filling in the center of each pasta circle. To fold each dumpling, using a fingertip, lightly moisten the edges of a pasta circle with water—just the smallest amount of water will do. Fold the pasta in half over the filling, forming a half circle, and eliminating any air pockets, firmly pinch the edges together to seal. Lightly moisten the corners of the pasta along the straight side of the half circle with water. Fold the two corners together and pinch firmly to seal, forming pudgy dumplings. Size varies.

Agnolotti: Using a piping bag fitted with a large plain tip, pipe large bite-size lengths of filling along the long side of a sheet of pasta, parallel to and about 1 inch (2.5 cm) in from the edge and leaving about a finger's width between each portion. Roll the edge of the pasta up and all the way around the filling to completely enclose it, then pinch the pasta at both ends of each portion of filling, eliminating any air pockets. Using a wheel cutter, cut away excess pasta and then cut between each portion of filling, forming pillow-shaped dumplings. Size and shape vary.

Fagottini: Cut the sheeted pasta into squares using a wheel cutter. Place a small amount of filling in the center of each pasta square. To fold each dumpling, using a fingertip, lightly moisten the edges of a pasta square with water—just the smallest amount of water will do. Bring all four corners of the pasta square together over the filling and, eliminating any air pockets, firmly pinch each of the four edges together to seal, forming pyramid-shaped dumplings. Size varies.

◄ Pelmeni

Tortelloni, Tortelli, Tortellini, and Wontons: Cut the sheeted pasta into squares using a wheel cutter. Place a small amount of filling in the center of each pasta square. To fold each dumpling, using a fingertip, lightly moisten the edges of a pasta square with water—just the smallest amount of water will do. Fold the pasta in half over the filling, forming a triangle, and eliminating any air pockets, firmly pinch the edges together to seal. Lightly moisten the corners of the pasta along the long side of the triangle with water. Fold the two corners together and pinch firmly to seal, forming pudgy dumplings. Size varies, though tortelloni are relatively large: perhaps 2¼-inch (6-cm) squares of pasta with 1 scant teaspoon of filling. Tortellini are tiny: 1¾-inch (4.5-cm) squares of pasta with ¼ teaspoon of filling.

Caramelle: Cut the sheeted pasta into squares using a wheel cutter. Place a small amount of filling in the center of each pasta square. To fold each dumpling, using a fingertip, lightly moisten one edge of a pasta square with water—just the smallest amount of water will do. Starting from the edge opposite the moistened side, roll the pasta up and all the way around the filling to completely enclose it, and eliminating any air pockets, firmly pinch or twist each end of the pasta in opposite directions to seal, forming dumplings in the shape of wrapped candies. Size varies.

SCRAP PASTA DOUGH

· · · · ·

Scraps from cutting and forming pasta sheets that haven't dried too much and are still supple can be brushed free of excess flour, kneaded together with a few drops of water, and then re-sheeted. Or they can be cooked as maltagliati.

Scraps leftover from laminating different colors of pasta are particularly good for re-sheeting as they create different beautiful marbled effects.

Maltagliati: Scraps from cutting other pasta shapes. *Maltagliati* means "badly cut" in Italian. Leave scraps as they are or cut them into smaller irregular pieces as desired. Good for soup.

◀ Tortelloni of Spinach Egg Pasta and Spinach-Ricotta Filling

KEEPING PREPARED PASTA FROM STICKING

. . . . . .

Arrange short-cut pasta as it is made in a single layer on pasta screens or flour sack towel–lined baking trays.

Dust long-cut pasta generously with flour as it is made and form loose nests on pasta screens or flour sack towel–lined baking trays. Alternatively, hang long-cut pasta on a pasta rack. Long-cut pasta that is hung dries more evenly, but nests are more manageable and easier to get into a pot of boiling water.

Stuffed pasta is the most likely to stick because moist fillings tend to soak through. So take extra care with stuffed pasta and arrange it as it is made in a single layer on flour sack towel–lined pasta screens or baking trays. Alternatively arrange it in a single layer on baking sheets with a heavy dusting of semolina. On the other hand, the corners and edges tend to dry out, so keep stuffed pasta covered with flour sack towels as you work.

Pasta may be cooked immediately or left at room temperature like this for several hours, except stuffed pasta which must be cooked within 2 or 3 hours or refrigerated for food safety. Pasta that has been allowed to dry for at least a couple of hours will hold its shape much better when boiled.

To keep pasta that's made in the morning moist until dinnertime, keep it covered with flour sack towels on flour sack towel–lined pasta screens or baking trays.

CLEANING THE SHEETER

. . . . . .

Cleaning the sheeter is as simple as brushing it off. Use a wooden skewer or toothpick to dislodge any stubborn bits of dough. It is okay to use a lightly moistened towel, but do not wash in running water or in the dishwasher.

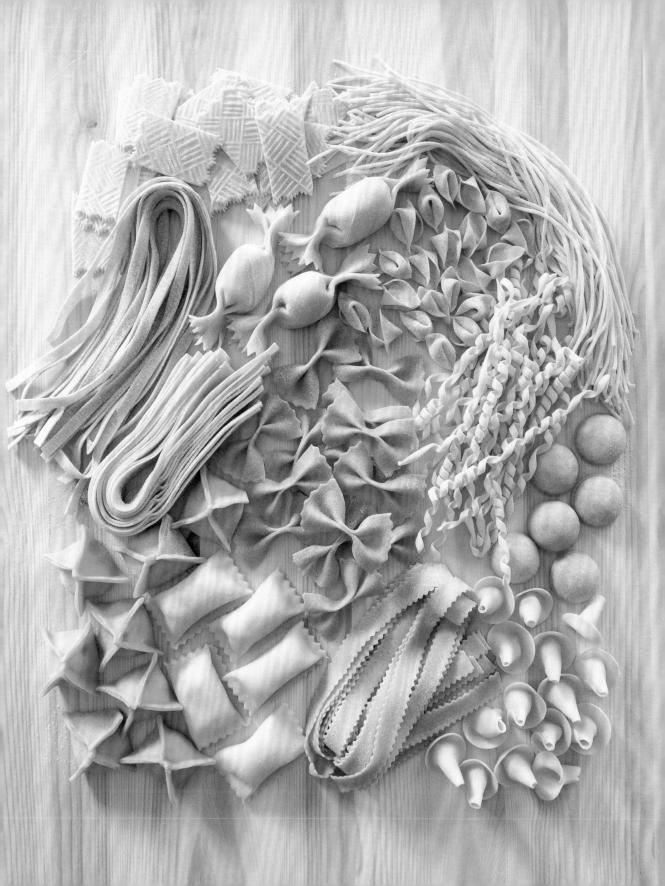

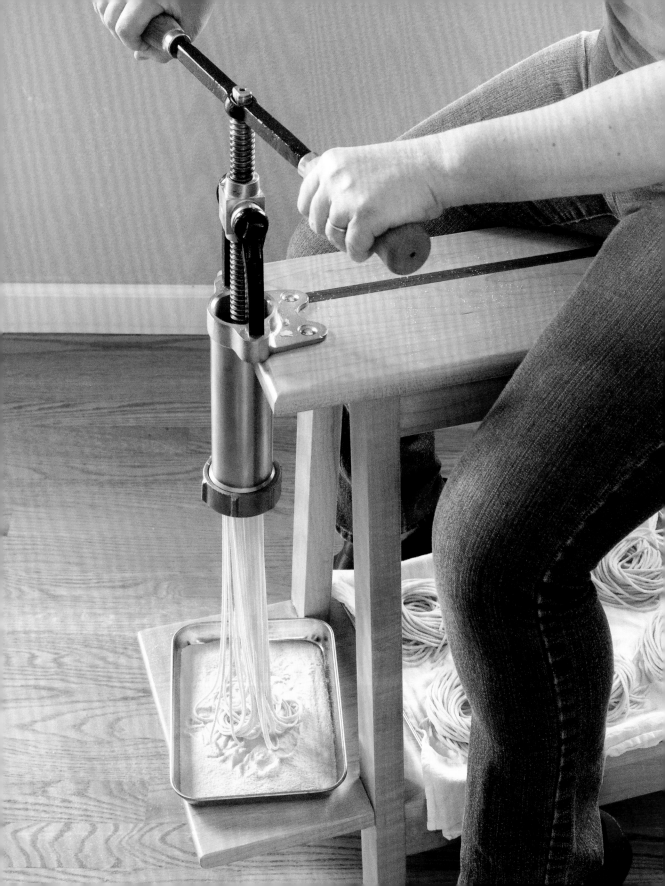

CHAPTER 2

Using the Extruder Pasta Machine

DOUGH RECIPES FOR THE EXTRUDER

· · · · · ·

BASIC EXTRUDER DOUGH FORMULATION

Use 33 grams (1⅛ ounces) of water per 100 grams (3½ ounces) of semolina, or 33% hydration, as a starting point.

Different types of extruders require different dough hydrations depending on how powerful they are, if they are electric or manual, and whether they employ an auger or piston design. Some electric commercial machines may take doughs with hydration levels of 30% or lower, while Bigolaro users may prefer the ease of cranking the machine with 40 to 45% hydration dough. Experiment and adjust accordingly. Different dies may also require slight adjustments in hydration for the different shapes to extrude properly.

Semolina Pasta

YIELDS 4 MAIN-COURSE SERVINGS

This is your basic extruder dough, with 33% hydration. It yields a firm pasta with a resilient chew. For pasta with a slightly finer texture, try with using semola rimacinata or even finely milled durum flour rather than semolina.

500 g (1 lb. 1⅔ oz) semolina

165 g (5¾ oz) water, preferably lukewarm

To mix the dough and prepare it for the machine, see page 82.

Tomato Variation: Use tomato paste for a hint of sweetness and a pale orange color. Blend 40 grams (1⅓ ounces) of tomato paste with the water before mixing the dough.

Sweet Chile Variation: For a lovely orange-colored dough with a hint of sweet chile flavor, use either sweet Calabrian chile, which is available at some gourmet grocers and online, or sweet Hungarian paprika. Blend 14 grams (½ ounce) of sweet Calabrian chile powder or 10 grams (⅓ ounce) of sweet Hungarian paprika with the semolina before mixing the dough. Hungarian paprika can sometimes have a hint of bitterness, so I use less.

(continued)

Sweet Chile Semolina Bucatini ▶

Pimenton Variation: Use pimenton, which is also known as smoked Spanish paprika, for an orange-colored dough with a subtle smoky flavor that's excellent paired with tomato sauces. Blend 9 grams (⅓ ounce) of pimenton with the semolina before mixing the dough.

Squid Ink Variation: Squid ink, which is available in tiny packets at fishmongers and gourmet grocers, makes for jet-black pasta with a hint of briny flavor. It's perfect with seafood sauces. Blend 7 grams (¼ ounce) of squid ink with the water before mixing the dough. Squid ink doesn't seem to want to dissolve easily, so start by loosening it up with just a spoonful of water before mixing it with the remaining quantity.

Saffron Semolina Pasta

YIELDS 4 MAIN-COURSE SERVINGS

This pasta is colored with saffron. It is especially delicious with seafood sauces and spicy pork or sausage ragus.

Several generous pinches saffron

165 g (5¾ oz) boiling water

500 g (1 lb. 1⅔ oz) semolina

Grind the saffron to a powder with mortar and pestle. Pour the boiling water over the saffron and let cool until lukewarm before mixing the dough. To mix the dough and prepare it for the machine, see page 82.

Egg Semolina Pasta

YIELDS 4 MAIN-COURSE SERVINGS

You can expect egg dough for the extruder to feel initially stickier than dough made with water. This is because it takes longer for semolina to hydrate with just egg alone. So be patient and try to resist the temptation to add semolina.

480 g (1 lb. 1 oz) semolina

4 eggs (230 g shelled), preferably at room temperature, blended

To mix the dough and prepare it for the machine, see page 82.

Whole Durum Pasta

YIELDS 4 MAIN-COURSE SERVINGS

This pasta is light brown in color with a bold, wheaty flavor. It has a slightly coarse texture and is noticeably less chewy than pasta made from semolina alone.

In terms of formulation, whole durum flour requires quite a bit more water than semolina. This dough is best suited for short-cut shapes. The bran in the whole durum flour interrupts gluten, so long-cut pastas are more prone to breakage.

500 g (1 lb. 1⅔ oz) whole durum flour

220 g (7¾ oz) water, preferably lukewarm

To mix the dough and prepare it for the machine, see page 82.

◀ Egg Semolina Trotolle and Egg Semolina Campanelle

INSTRUCTIONS FOR THE EXTRUDER

· · · · · ·

USING THE EXTRUDER'S INTEGRATED MIXER TO MIX THE DOUGH

Blend the dry ingredients in the extruder's mixing chamber. Blend together all of the wet ingredients. With the motor running, slowly trickle in the wet ingredients a tiny bit at a time until completely absorbed and the mixture resembles wet sand. This should take a good 8 to 10 minutes. A cohesive dough will not form, but it should hold together when squeezed. If the dough does not hold together when squeezed, add a little splash of water and mix a minute longer.

USING A STAND MIXER TO MIX DOUGH FOR THE EXTRUDER

Blend the dry ingredients in a mixer fitted with a paddle attachment. Blend together all of the wet ingredients. With the motor running on low speed, slowly trickle in the wet ingredients a tiny bit at a time until completely absorbed and the mixture resembles wet sand. This should take a good 8 to 10 minutes. A cohesive dough will not form, but it should hold together when squeezed. If the dough does not hold together when squeezed, add a little splash of water and mix a minute longer. Cover the bowl tightly with plastic wrap unless you are using a Bigolaro.

For the Bigolaro, squeeze and knead the dough right in the mixer bowl until it holds together then divide and shape it into portions that will fit inside the barrel of the machine. Wrap each portion tightly in plastic wrap to keep it from drying out.

RESTING THE DOUGH
FOR THE EXTRUDER

Commercial machines and machines with electric motors can extrude the dough immediately after mixing. For manual machines, I prefer to let the dough rest at room temperature for at least an hour and preferably two. The resting time allows the flour to fully hydrate.

EXTRUDING THE PASTA
WITH THE MACHINE

Fit the machine with the desired die. Forming the pasta is as simple as passing the dough through the machine.

For auger-type machines, feed the crumbly dough loosely into the extruder. Do not compact it, or it might bind in the hopper and not feed into the auger. Extrude the pasta, cutting it when it reaches the desired length using the machine's integrated cutter or a paring knife or bench scraper.

For the Bigolaro, drop one portion of dough into the machine. Extrude the pasta, cutting it when it reaches the desired length using a paring knife or bench scraper. To prevent "blow outs" completely extrude one portion of dough, making sure the piston makes it all the way to the die and can go no further, before adding the next portion. For short-cut pasta, work with a partner or it may be easier and more efficient to make short-cut pasta by extruding it quite long and then cutting it to the desired length using a knife on a board.

Misshapen pasta, which happens from time to time, can be added back to the dough and extruded again.

EXTRUDED PASTA SHAPES

There are countless extruded pasta shapes. Here are a few of the most common ones. Doubtless you are familiar with most if not all of them.

Spaghetti: Round pasta strands

Angel Hair and Capellini: Thin round pasta strands, like thin spaghetti

Linguine: Oval pasta strands

Fettuccine: Pasta ribbons

Reginette and Mafaldine: Wide pasta ribbons with ruffled edges

Lasagna: Pasta sheets with ruffled edges

Bucatini: Hollow round pasta strands, like thick spaghetti with a hole in the center

Macaroni: Short-cut pasta tubes, sometimes curved or elbow-shaped

Rigatoni: Short-cut ridged pasta tubes

Penne: Short-cut quill-shaped pasta, or pasta tubes cut on a bias. There is a special cone-shaped penne die but you can also cheat by using a rigatoni die, extruding the pasta quite long, and then cutting it on a bias using a knife on a board.

Paccheri: Large short-cut pasta tubes

Ziti: Long-cut pasta tubes

Anellini: Little pasta rings, like SpaghettiOs

Fusilli and Rotini: Corkscrew or helix-shaped pasta

Spaghetti Quadri and Chitarra: Square pasta strands, like square spaghetti

Casarecce and Gemilli: Twisted S-shaped pasta strands

Lumache: Snail-shaped pasta

Trottole: Spinning top-shaped pasta

Campanelle: Bell-shaped pasta

Radiatore: Radiator-shaped pasta

EXTRUDED PASTA BLENDS

Mista Corta: A blend of short-cut shapes, such as reginette, macaroni, fusilli, and casarecce

Mista Lunga: A blend of long-cut shapes, such as spaghetti, fettuccine, reginette, bucatini

Mista corta and mista lunga are meant to replicate the blends created by frugal Italian nonnas, who would artfully combine the small quantities of different shapes of pasta leftover in the bottom of various packages. Pasta shapes are blended with great care and consideration for pairing with the selected sauce.

KEEPING PREPARED PASTA
FROM STICKING

· · · · ·

Arrange short-cut pasta as it is made in a single layer on pasta screens or flour sack towel–lined baking trays.

Dust long-cut pasta generously with semolina as it is made and form loose nests on pasta screens or flour sack towel–lined baking trays. Alternatively, hang long-cut pasta on a pasta rack. Long-cut pasta that is hung dries more evenly, but nests are more manageable and easier to get into a pot of boiling water.

Pasta may be cooked immediately or left at room temperature like this for up to several hours. Pasta that has been allowed to dry for at least a couple of hours will hold its shape much better when boiled.

To keep pasta that's made in the morning moist until dinnertime, keep it covered with flour sack towels on flour sack towel–lined pasta screens or baking trays.

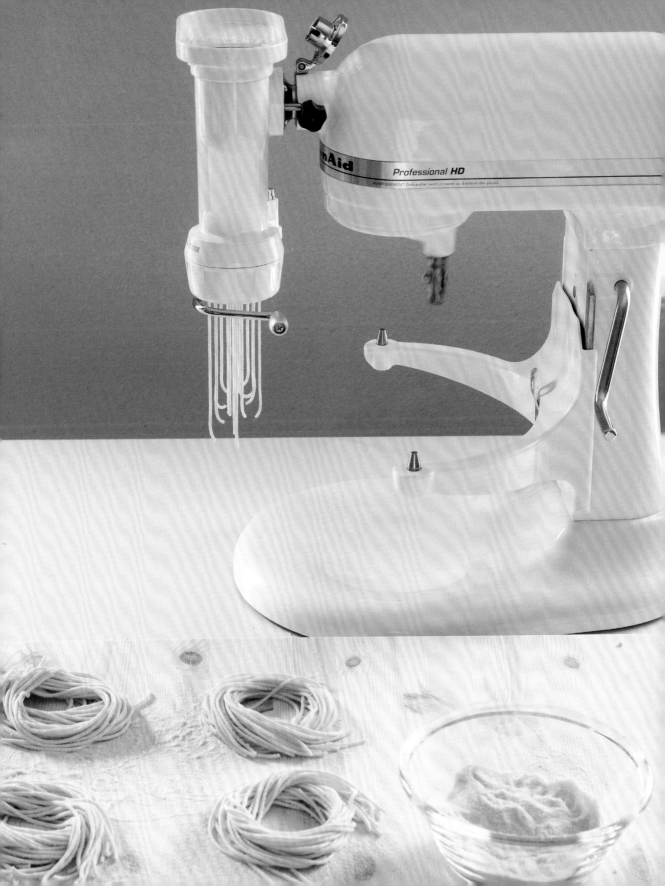

CLEANING THE EXTRUDER

· · · · ·

To clean commercial extruders, follow manufacturer instructions. To clean the home extruder, disassemble it completely. Remove any large globs of dough. Leave everything else except bronze dies to air dry. Then simply brush clean; dry bits of dough will pop out or flake right off aluminum and plastic. It is okay to use a lightly moistened towel, but do not wash with running water or in the dishwasher.

To clean a bronze die, soak it in water overnight. Then wash carefully, using a toothpick to dislodge stubborn bits of dough. Use water pressure to help rinse away dough as it's loosened and dissolved; I've heard of people even resorting to Waterpiks. Do not use brushes or other similar tools; you risk damaging the die because bronze is relatively soft. I usually soak mine for a while, work at it a while, and repeat. I'm not even gonna lie, this part is a pain. But homemade bronze-extruded pasta is totally worth it!

If you use your extruder on a daily basis, do like the pros do and simply store your bronze dies submerged in water, possibly in the refrigerator. Just change the water frequently to keep it from getting gross. Whenever you make pasta, simply discard the first bit of dough that gets extruded.

CHAPTER 3

Using the Cavatelli Maker Pasta Machine

DOUGH RECIPES FOR THE CAVATELLI MAKER

· · · · ·

BASIC CAVATELLI MAKER DOUGH FORMULATION

Use 50 grams (1¾ ounces) of water per 100 grams (3½ ounces) of semolina, or 50% hydration.

Cavatelli

YIELDS 4 MAIN-COURSE SERVINGS

This is a 50% hydration dough. It's a pleasure to work with: supple and extensible with minimal sticking.

500 g (1 lb. 1⅔ oz) semolina

250 g (8¾ oz) water, preferably lukewarm

To mix the dough and prepare it for the machine, see page 96.

Tomato Variation: Use tomato paste for a hint of sweetness and a pale orange color. Blend 40 grams (1⅓ ounces) of tomato paste with the water before mixing the dough.

Sweet Chile Variation: For a lovely orange-colored dough with a hint of sweet chile flavor, use either sweet Calabrian chile, which is available at some gourmet grocers and online, or sweet Hungarian paprika. Blend 14 grams (½ ounce) of sweet Calabrian chile powder or 10 grams (⅓ ounce) of sweet Hungarian paprika with the semolina before mixing the dough. Hungarian paprika can sometimes have a hint of bitterness, so I use less.

Pimenton Variation: Use pimenton, which is also known as smoked Spanish paprika, for an orange-colored dough with a subtle smoky flavor that's excellent paired with tomato sauces. Blend 9 grams (⅓ ounce) of pimenton with the semolina before mixing the dough.

Cavatelli ▶

Butternut Squash Cavatelli

YIELDS 4 MAIN-COURSE SERVINGS

This chewy pasta has the deep orange color, sweet aroma, and flavor of butternut squash. Serve it simply with Sage Brown Butter (page 110) or double up on the squash and use it to make Pasta with Italian Sausage, Butternut Squash, and Sage (page 174).

½ medium (about 515 g [1 lb. 2 oz]) butternut squash, halved and seeded

500 g (1 lb. 1⅔ oz) semolina

70 g (2½ oz) water

Preheat the oven to 400°F (200°C, or gas mark 6).

Bake the squash cut-side down on a baking sheet for 30 minutes. Flip the squash and bake until tender to the center when tested with a paring knife, about 45 minutes. Let cool.

When the squash is cool enough to handle, scoop the flesh out of the skin and purée it using a ricer or food mill. Let cool to room temperature.

Use 240 grams (8½ ounces) of the squash purée to mix the dough. Reserve the remaining squash purée for another use. To mix the dough and prepare it for the machine, see page 96.

Ancient Wheat Cavatelli

YIELDS 4 MAIN-COURSE SERVINGS

If you're really into making pasta at home, it can be fun to experiment with different types of whole wheat and particularly einkorn, emmer, Khorasan, also known as Kamut, and spelt, all of which predate the modern varieties on the market today. It's quite interesting to experience the differences in color, hydration, aroma, and of course flavor. Khorasan cavatelli is blonde, while cavatelli made from emmer is the darkest. Einkorn and emmer require relatively little water, or they become unmanageably sticky. And as far as flavor goes, einkorn has an intriguing caramel-like sweetness; emmer and spelt are complex and earthy and can sometimes have a bitterness; Khorasan has a straightforward nuttiness.

Note that the bran in whole wheat flour interrupts gluten, so whole wheat cavatelli is noticeably less chewy than cavatelli made with semolina.

EINKORN CAVATELLI

500 g (1 lb. 1⅔ oz) whole einkorn flour

212 g (4½ oz) water, preferably lukewarm

EMMER CAVATELLI

500 g (1 lb. 1⅔ oz) whole emmer flour

212 g (4½ oz) water, preferably lukewarm

KHORASAN CAVATELLI

500 g (1 lb. 1⅔ oz) whole Khorasan flour

250 g (8¾ oz) water, preferably lukewarm

SPELT CAVATELLI

500 g (1 lb. 1⅔ oz) whole spelt flour

250 g (8¾ oz) water, preferably lukewarm

To mix the dough and prepare it for the machine, see page 96.

Grano Arso Cavatelli

YIELDS 4 MAIN-COURSE SERVINGS

Grano arso means "burnt grain" in Italian. The use of burnt grain for making pasta is likely to have originated hundreds of years ago in the cuisine of poverty in southern Italy. While burnt or toasted grain may no longer be a necessity for survival, it is still delicious. Toasted semolina gives cavatelli a brown color and slightly grainy texture. The flavor is deep and toasty, reminiscent of the dark, deeply caramelized crust of an artisan pizza or loaf of bread.

Toasting degrades gluten, so only a fraction of the semolina is toasted for grano arso pasta. The dough will seem a bit coarse and crumbly at first, but it will come together with vigorous kneading.

You can experiment with baking the semolina up to 2 and even 3 hours, until it is quite dark and just begins to smoke. If you do so, you may find that the dough requires an extra few drops of water. The pasta will have an even more pronounced toasted flavor and a hint of bitterness.

Pair a boldly flavored sauce with this boldly flavored pasta.

500 g (1 lb. 1⅔ oz) semolina

250 g (8¾ oz) water, preferably lukewarm

Preheat the oven to 350°F (175°C, or gas mark 4).

Spread 125 grams (4½ ounces) of the semolina on a baking tray and bake until toasted and golden brown, about 1 hour. Let cool to room temperature and sift through a fine-mesh sieve before blending with the remaining semolina and mixing the dough. To mix the dough and prepare it for the machine, see page 96.

Malloreddus

YIELDS 4 MAIN-COURSE SERVINGS

These small golden dumplings, also known as gnocchetti Sardi or Sardinian gnocchi, are often colored with saffron.

Malloreddus is especially delicious with spicy pork or sausage ragus.

250 g (8¾ oz) boiling water

Several generous pinches saffron

500 g (1 lb. 1⅔ oz) semolina

Pour the boiling water over the saffron and let cool until lukewarm before mixing the dough. To mix the dough and prepare it for the machine, see page 96.

INSTRUCTIONS FOR THE CAVATELLI MAKER

· · · · ·

MIXING AND KNEADING DOUGH FOR THE CAVATELLI MAKER BY HAND

Mixing pasta dough by hand for the cavatelli maker is quite easy and straightforward. Blend the dry ingredients, add the wet ingredients, and mix until a rough dough forms. Some cooks prefer to do this in the Italian style directly on a wooden board, making a mound of flour with a well in the center, adding the wet ingredients into the well, and then bringing the dough together using a fork. Other cooks prefer to mix the dough in a large, broad bowl using just their hands. Cooks using the well method stir the flour into the water gradually, while others mix the water all through the flour from the get-go.

Mixing by hand is my own preferred method of making dough for the cavatelli maker because it's easy and generates the least dirty dishes. I usually mix in a bowl with just my hands, though sometimes I do it using a pair of cooking chopsticks. I like to mix the wet ingredients all through the dry ingredients, distributing them as evenly as possible. This creates lots of small shaggy bits that I then squeeze and press firmly together and into any loose dry ingredients at the bottom of the bowl to pick them up. I suggest you experiment with the different approaches and decide which is most comfortable for you.

The amount of flour needed may vary slightly depending on the brand of the flour and the humidity. Keep in mind that it's much easier to add flour to a wet dough than it is to add liquid to a dry dough, so you can hold back a bit of the flour at first and then add more if the dough feels sticky. You're after a firm dough that's just barely sticky. A bit of tension between the machine and the dough is what causes the dough to curl up into cavatelli.

Although it is possible to mix dough for the cavatelli maker in the food processor or stand mixer, I can't recommend it. The dough is really too firm for either of these machines to fully develop and several minutes of kneading by hand would still be required. So why bother? (Unlike the pasta sheeter, the cavatelli maker does not complete gluten development.)

If you've mixed your dough in a bowl, transfer it to a wooden work surface now.

Knead the dough until it is smooth and elastic, about 10 minutes. Kneading will be a little bit of a workout. If you or the dough need a break, by which I mean the dough feels resistant to kneading or seems to be tearing, wrap the dough in plastic wrap or cover with an inverted bowl and let rest for a few minutes. Kneading should be much easier once you come back to it. The dough is ready when it springs back readily when poked. If there are any dry bits of dough on the kneading surface, take care to avoid working them into the dough.

Wrap the dough tightly in plastic wrap to keep it from drying out.

RESTING THE DOUGH FOR THE CAVATELLI MAKER

Let the dough rest at room temperature for at least an hour and preferably two. The resting time allows the flour to fully hydrate.

MAKING DOUGH FOR THE CAVATELLI MAKER IN ADVANCE

At this point you can refrigerate the wrapped pasta dough for 24 to 48 hours. Bring refrigerated pasta dough to room temperature before shaping.

SHAPING THE PASTA WITH THE CAVATELLI MAKER

Work quickly to prevent the pasta from drying out. Do not use dusting flour. Cut the dough in half and rewrap 1 portion to keep it from drying out. Using a rolling pin, roll the other portion of dough to a thickness of just under ½ inch (1 cm). Cut the dough into strips that are all the same width and somewhat narrower than the rollers of the machine, ¾ inch (2 cm) wide is a pretty good size. Pass each strip of dough through the machine, cranking the handle slowly to form the cavatelli. Make more cavatelli with the remaining portion of dough in the same manner.

The size of the cavatelli will vary depending on the width of the strips of dough.

Scraps and misshapen cavatelli, which happen from time to time, can be kneaded together and then formed again.

Forming Other Cavatelli Maker Pasta Shapes

Orecchiette: Turn each cavatelli shell inside out before the pasta has a chance to dry, forming ear-shaped pasta.

Malloreddus, Gnocchetti Sardi, and Sardinian Gnocchi: Cut strips of pasta to pass through the machine ½ inch (1 cm) or narrower, forming tiny cavatelli shells.

Try to make all of the cavatelli, orecchiette, or malloreddus within each batch the same thickness and size so that they cook evenly.

TROUBLESHOOTING

· · · · · ·

Dough must be the right consistency for the cavatelli maker to work.

If dough smears out inside the roof of the machine and sticks there, it is too wet. Knead in a large pinch of flour and try shaping it again. Just flouring the dough is not helpful as it will just slip through the machine without curling up into cavatelli.

If dough passes through the machine without curling up into cavatelli, it is too dry. If the dough worked in the cavatelli maker initially but then stopped curling up later in the batch, the surface has dried too much. Keep the strips of dough covered as you work. If the dough doesn't curl up from the get-go, knead in a few drops of water at a time until it works. Also avoid using dusting flour; it can cause dough to slip through the machine without curling.

KEEPING PREPARED PASTA FROM STICKING

· · · · · ·

Arrange cavatelli and orecchiette as they are made in a single layer on pasta screens or flour sack towel–lined baking trays.

Cavatelli and orecchiette may be cooked immediately or left at room temperature like this for up to several hours.

To keep cavatelli that's made in the morning moist until dinnertime, keep it covered with flour sack towels on flour sack towel–lined pasta screens or baking trays.

CLEANING THE CAVATELLI MAKER

· · · · · ·

Cleaning the cavatelli maker is as simple as brushing it off. Use a wooden skewer or toothpick to dislodge any stubborn bits of dough. It is okay to use a lightly moistened towel, but do not wash with running water or in the dishwasher.

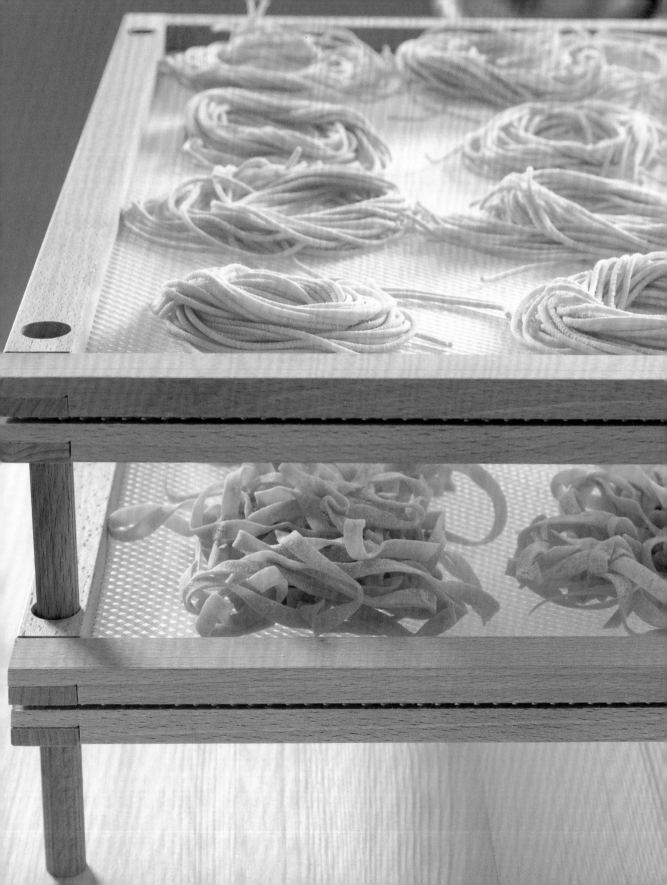

CHAPTER 4

Storing, Cooking, Saucing, and Serving Fresh Pasta and Noodles

STORING FRESH PASTA AND NOODLES

· · · · ·

Most likely you'll want to consume your homemade fresh pasta and noodles fresh, that is, the same day you make them. It is, however, possible to make pasta in advance and store it with excellent results.

REFRIGERATING AND FREEZING FRESH PASTA AND NOODLES

To refrigerate or freeze fresh pasta and noodles, first check that they're either sufficiently dried on the surface or dusted with enough flour to keep from sticking. Arrange the pasta in an even layer on a flour sack towel–lined baking tray, cover it with another flour sack towel, and wrap the entire tray tightly in plastic wrap to keep it from drying out. The towels keep condensation off the pasta.

To freeze filled pasta, stack it between sheets of parchment on a baking tray. Transfer it to a large zip-top bag once frozen solid.

Pasta and noodles containing a large amount of egg will keep for a day or two refrigerated. Frozen, they'll keep for a week or two. Pasta and noodles containing little or no egg are less prone to oxidation and will keep for up to three or four days refrigerated and a month or more frozen. Do not thaw frozen pasta before cooking but adjust the cooking time accordingly.

DRYING FRESH PASTA AND NOODLES

If you should have leftovers or the occasion to give a gift of pasta, you may want to experiment with drying it. You might think it's a simple as leaving the pasta on the pasta rack until it's bone dry. But drying pasta at the ambient temperature and humidity of the home kitchen can sometimes lead to inconsistent results. Commercial manufacturers have climate controlled chambers specifically designed for drying pasta.

Cracking is a common problem. I have encountered it myself, and let me tell you it is quite frustrating to find the pasta that you labored over has crumbled into pieces. The good news is I believe I have cracked the cracking. My theory is that in a relatively dry environment, cracking occurs because the surface of pasta dries before the center. The solution is to slow surface drying so that the pasta can dry from the center, which can be accomplished by drying pasta covered with flour sack towels on flour sack towel–lined pasta screens overnight. Dying time will vary according to the thickness of the pasta and the humidity in the air, but it shouldn't take so long that the pasta begins to mold. Check that the pasta is completely dry by breaking a piece—it should shatter readily.

Dried pasta and noodles will keep for several months tightly sealed in the pantry. Cooking time of dried pasta is significantly longer than that of fresh pasta.

BOILING AND SAUCING
FRESH PASTA AND NOODLES

· · · · ·

Boiling homemade fresh pasta and noodles is essentially the same as boiling any dry store-bought variety, except cooking time is shorter.

Fill a large pot with water. An abundant quantity of water is necessary so that it returns to a boil as quickly as possible once the pasta is added and the pasta cooks as quickly as possible. Pasta that is cooked slowly is more likely to become overcooked and mushy. Also the pot should have enough headspace to allow for displacement and the bubbling of the water. An 8-quart (7.6-liter) stockpot with 6 quarts (5.7 liters) of water is just right for boiling one recipe of pasta. Bring the water to a full rolling boil, then salt generously with 2 to 3 tablespoons (36 to 55 grams) of kosher salt for 6 quarts (5.7 liters) of water. Pasta is bland and salty cooking water is necessary to season it through and through. There's no need to add any oil to the water.

Have a colander or wire skimmer at the ready before you start boiling the pasta.

Add the pasta or noodles to the boiling water—if the pasta was laid out on a flour sack towel, then it's convenient to pick up the towel by the corners and use it to transport and dump the entire batch into the pot. Return the water to a boil over high heat. Stir frequently, especially until the water returns to a boil, to keep the pasta from sticking together and to the bottom of the pot. Strands of ribbon pastas and noodles are the most likely to stick because they have the most surface area to make contact, so pay close attention to those.

Cook pasta and noodles at a full boil until the desired doneness, just shy of al dente for pasta and just tender for noodles. *Al dente*, which translates to "to the tooth," means that the pasta is cooked through but still has a firm bite. Test for doneness early and often by tasting a little piece. (No flinging food at the walls, please!) By the way, floating is a good indicator that the pasta is nearly done.

SUGGESTED FRESH PASTA AND NOODLE COOKING TIMES

Fresh pasta and noodles cook in just minutes. Cooking times will vary according to thickness and how much they have dried, but the following chart gives a good idea of timing.

FRESH PASTA/ NOODLE TYPE	SUGGESTED COOKING TIME
Fresh sheeted pasta shapes	2 to 4 minutes
Fresh extruded pasta shapes	4 minutes
Fresh cavatelli machine shapes	5 to 6 minutes
Any fresh shapes to be used in baked pasta dishes, such as lasagna	30 seconds (parcook only)

Before draining pasta, reserve a generous ladleful of the pasta cooking water.

If the pasta is to be combined with the sauce on the heat, drain it when it is nearly al dente, transfer it to the sauce, and simmer while tossing gently to coat—these last few moments of cooking will finish the pasta to a perfect al dente and at the same time marry the pasta and sauce into one cohesive dish. If the pasta is to be combined with the sauce off the heat, drain it when it is very nearly al dente, transfer it to the sauce, and toss gently to coat—residual heat, or carryover cooking, will finish the pasta to perfection.

As you toss the pasta with the sauce, thin with the reserved pasta water as desired. Salty, starchy pasta water not only thins the sauce but also gives it flavor and body and helps to emulsify it so that it clings well to the pasta. Pasta cooking water is a valuable ingredient, so don't just flush it all down the drain when you pour your pasta into a colander in the sink.

Do not rinse pasta before tossing it with the sauce or you will wash away all the precious starch from its surface. One of the only exception is if the pasta is destined for a cold dish such as pasta salad—in that case, shock the pasta to stop the cooking as quickly as possible by rinsing it with cold water.

A FEW LAST THOUGHTS ON SAUCE FOR FRESH PASTA

- Timing is key when cooking pasta. The pasta and sauce must be done at the same time, which can be tricky especially when making quick stovetop sauces. So here's my strategy to have perfectly al dente pasta every time: I'd rather the sauce wait on the pasta than the pasta wait on the sauce. In other words, err on the side of having the sauce done early and keep it warm at the ready. The quality of the sauce likely won't degrade, but keeping pasta hot for any length of time will cause it to turn mushy.

- When making cheese sauces, I prefer to add the cheese off the heat and let it melt from residual heat alone. Cooking cheese on the heat can result in a grainy texture.

- Be careful when seasoning pasta sauces with salt. Undersalt a skosh to account for the addition of pasta cooking water and Parmigiano or Pecorino, which are all relatively salty ingredients.

- Toss delicate shapes, such as garganelli and ravioli and other stuffed pastas, with sauce very gently to avoid breaking.

- Ragus and other braised or stewed pasta sauces get better with time. So consider making these a day or two ahead and reheat before combining with pasta to serve.

- Each of the countless pasta shapes pairs best with a particular sauce. I make recommendations in the recipes for the finished dishes, but feel free to mix and match as you like.

FRYING AND SAUCING
FRESH PASTA AND NOODLES

· · · · ·

Fresh pasta and noodles may be fried as well as boiled. For instance, you can make pasta chips by simply frying pasta triangles and seasoning them with salt or cinnamon-sugar. Fried wontons (page 149), fried ravioli, and cannoli (page 181) are other popular examples.

Many pasta and noodle shapes, such as wontons, are fried naked. Ravioli is usually breaded before frying. To bread dumplings, coat each one with seasoned flour, then seasoned egg wash, which is egg thinned with water or milk, and finally seasoned breadcrumbs. This three-step procedure is necessary to make the breading adhere.

Add enough neutral frying oil, such as vegetable or canola, to a large, heavy pot to submerge a batch of pasta by a couple of inches. You'll want to fry the pasta or noodles in batches so as not to overcrowd the oil and cause the oil temperature to

drop precipitously. Heat the oil to 350 to 375°F (175 to 190°C).

Have a wire skimmer, a paper towel–lined baking tray, and any necessary seasonings such as salt or cinnamon-sugar at the ready before you start frying the pasta.

Add the pasta or noodles to the oil and fry, stirring frequently, until the pasta is golden brown and the bubbling begins to subside. Floating is a good indicator that the pasta is nearly done. Using the wire skimmer, remove the pasta to the towel-lined baking tray and let it drain for a few moments. If the pasta is to be sprinkled with salt or rolled in cinnamon-sugar, do it as soon as it comes out of the oil or it won't stick.

Serve the pasta with any dipping sauce on the side.

To avoid a safety hazard, after frying leave the pot of hot oil on the stovetop undisturbed to cool completely and only then clean up.

SERVING FRESH PASTA AND NOODLES

· · · · ·

You can serve pasta family-style piled high on a big platter in the center of the table, or you can twirl it around a meat fork in a ladle and plate it restaurant style.

Whether you choose to go casual or fancy, don't forget to garnish. Freshly grated Parmigiano or Pecorino are requisite garnishes for many pasta dishes. A sprinkling of minced fresh herbs or a drizzle of extra-virgin olive oil may be in order too.

CHAPTER 5

Creating Finished Dishes

Once you've learned how to make and cook fresh pasta and noodles from scratch, some solid finished dish recipes are in order. Here's a selection that'll take you all around the world. With everything from carbonara to tuna noodle and ramen to cannoli, it demonstrates the versatility and deliciousness of the humble noodle.

ESSENTIAL SAUCES

· · · · ·

Simple Tomato Sauce

YIELDS APPROXIMATELY 6½ CUPS (1.6 L), ENOUGH TO SAUCE 2 RECIPES OF PASTA, MAKING 8 SERVINGS

This is an easy and relatively quick-cooking all-purpose tomato sauce. Use it to sauce any pasta. The bright acidity of the tomatoes makes it especially nice with tortelloni with rich Spinach-Ricotta Filling (page 62).

This sauce keeps quite well in the refrigerator or freezer, so the recipe makes enough for a couple of pasta dinners.

3 tablespoons (45 ml) extra-virgin olive oil

1 yellow onion, diced

4 cloves garlic, minced

Generous pinch red chile flakes

2 cans (28 oz [794 g]) whole peeled tomatoes, preferably San Marzanos

1 large handful (about ¾ oz [20 g]) basil leaves, torn if large

Kosher salt

Freshly ground black pepper

Heat a large, heavy pot over medium-low heat until hot. Add the olive oil and swirl to coat the inside of the pan. Add the onion and sauté until soft, about 8 minutes. Add the garlic and chile flakes and sauté until fragrant, about 30 seconds. Add the tomatoes along with their liquid and the basil. Simmer, stirring occasionally and breaking up the tomatoes with the back of a spoon, until thickened, about 40 minutes. Purée using a stick blender, if desired. Season with salt and pepper.

Slow-Simmered Tomato Sauce

YIELDS APPROXIMATELY 7 CUPS (1.7 L), ENOUGH TO SAUCE 2 RECIPES OF PASTA,
MAKING 8 SERVINGS

Use this recipe when you want a deep, rich cooked-all-day sort of flavor. It's the perfect base
for Spaghetti alla Chittara with Meatballs (page 130), Spaghetti with Seafood Marinara
(page 162), and Pappardelle with Sunday Pork Ragu (page 118).

This sauce keeps quite well in the refrigerator or freezer, so the recipe makes enough for
a couple of pasta dinners.

¼ cup (60 ml) extra-virgin olive oil

1 yellow onion, diced small

1 stalk celery, diced small

1 small carrot, diced small

4 cloves garlic, minced

Generous pinch red chile flakes

2 tablespoons (32 g) tomato paste

2 cans (28 oz [794 g]) whole peeled
tomatoes, preferably San Marzanos

1 large handful (about ¾ oz
[20 g]) basil leaves, torn if large

3 sprigs oregano

1 small piece Parmigiano-Reggiano
rind, optional

Kosher salt

Freshly ground black pepper

Heat a large, heavy pot over medium-low heat until hot. Add the olive oil and swirl to coat the inside of the pan. Add the onion and sauté until extremely soft and translucent, about 10 minutes. Add the celery and carrot and sauté until soft, about 8 minutes. Add the garlic and chile flakes and sauté until fragrant, about 2 minutes. Add the tomato paste and sauté until golden brown, about 3 minutes. Add the canned tomatoes along with their liquid, basil, oregano, and Parmigiano rind, if desired. Bring to a boil and simmer slowly, stirring occasionally and breaking up the tomatoes with the back of a spoon, until thickened and orange in color, which indicates that the olive oil has emulsified into the sauce, about 2 hours. Discard the Parmigiano rind and purée using a stick blender. Season with salt and pepper.

Sage Brown Butter

YIELDS A SCANT ½ CUP (120 ML), ENOUGH TO SAUCE 1 RECIPE FRESH PASTA, MAKING 4 SERVINGS

Butter cooked until it is brown and nutty and infused with sage is an excellent sauce for ravioli with any ricotta or squash filling and for Butternut Squash Cavatelli (page 94).

1 stick (8 tablespoons [112 g]) unsalted butter, diced

1 handful (⅓ oz [10 g]) sage leaves

Kosher salt

Freshly ground black pepper

Heat a small, heavy saucepan over medium heat until hot. Add the butter and cook, stirring constantly, until golden brown, about 5 minutes. Remove from the heat, add the sage, and stir until the bubbling subsides. Season with salt and pepper.

Ravioli of Egg Pasta and Butternut Squash Filling with Sage Brown Butter ▶

THE ULTIMATE PASTA MACHINE COOKBOOK

Basil Pesto

YIELDS APPROXIMATELY 1 CUP (240 ML), ENOUGH TO SAUCE 1 RECIPE FRESH PASTA, MAKING 4 SERVINGS

Pesto made in a food processor is fine, but pesto made the traditional way in a mortar and pestle is transcendent. It has a creamy texture, the flavor is bright and clean, and it stays a vibrant green without turning black. So if you're going to take the time and effort to make pasta from scratch, why not elevate your pesto game too?

Toss this pesto with some freshly cooked pasta, along with a splash of pasta cooking water, and you've got a delicious meal. Toss in some fresh mozzarella pearls and halved ripe tomatoes and you've got a feast!

2 to 3 cloves garlic, sliced

¼ cup (35 g) pine nuts

3 to 4 large handfuls (2 to 3 oz [55 to 85 g]) basil leaves

Coarse sea salt

1½ oz (40 g) freshly grated Parmigiano-Reggiano

½ oz (15 g) freshly grated Pecorino Romano

¼ cup (60 ml) extra-virgin olive oil

Pound and grind the garlic to a paste in a large mortar and pestle. Add the pine nuts, then the basil a handful at a time and a small pinch of salt, and then the cheeses, pounding and grinding to a paste after each addition. Stir in the olive oil.

Ragu Bolognese

YIELDS A GENEROUS 8 CUPS (1.9 L), ENOUGH TO SAUCE 2 RECIPES FRESH PASTA,
MAKING 8 TO 10 SERVINGS

This is a slow-simmered thick, hearty meat sauce, light on the tomato, and very much like the ragus I've eaten at the source in Bologna. It's one of my all-time favorite pasta sauces. There's almost nothing better than fresh Egg Tagliatelle with Ragu Bolognese and plenty of Parmigiano, with the exception of the ultimate expression of pasta love, Lasagna Bolognese (page 115).

Traditionally this type of ragu is made with finely diced beef. A great shortcut to all that dicing is using coarsely ground beef. Ask your butcher for chili grind, which is just about perfect for the job.

3 oz (85 g) minced pancetta

3 tablespoons (45 ml) extra-virgin olive oil

1 yellow onion, diced small

3 stalks celery, diced small

1 carrot, diced small

6 cloves garlic, minced

¼ cup (64 g) tomato paste

3 lb. (1,360 g) 80% lean coarse ground beef, broken up

⅓ cup (80 ml) red wine

1 cup (240 ml) whole milk

3 cups (705 ml) Simple Beef Stock (page 196)

1 can (14½ oz [411 g]) diced tomatoes

1 bay leaf

Generous pinch freshly ground nutmeg

Freshly ground black pepper

Kosher salt

Heat a large, heavy pot over medium heat until hot. Add the pancetta and sauté until golden brown, about 6 minutes. Lower the heat to medium-low and add the olive oil and onion. Sauté until extremely soft and translucent, about 8 minutes. Add the celery and carrot and sauté until soft, about 9 minutes. Add the garlic and sauté until fragrant, about 2 minutes. Add the tomato paste and sauté until golden brown, about 3 minutes. Increase the heat to medium-high and add the ground beef. Cook, stirring frequently, until no longer pink, about 8 minutes. Add the wine and simmer, stirring occasionally, until nearly dry, about 6 minutes. Add the milk and simmer, stirring occasionally, until nearly dry, about 12 minutes. Add the stock, tomatoes along with their liquid, bay leaf, nutmeg, and a generous grinding of pepper, bring to a boil, and simmer slowly, stirring occasionally, until thickened, about 3 hours. Discard the bay leaf, skim off the fat as desired, and season with salt and pepper.

Béchamel Sauce

YIELDS APPROXIMATELY 7½ CUPS (1.8 L), ENOUGH TO SAUCE 2 RECIPES FRESH PASTA, MAKING 8 SERVINGS

This is your basic white sauce. Use it to make Lasagna Bolognese (page 115) and Tuna Noodle Casserole (page 119). Or add lots of grated cheese and pasta cooked until it's beginning to soften, along with a bit of mustard powder and a dash of both hot sauce and Worcestershire sauce, and bake it in a casserole dish, and you have mac and cheese.

1 stick (8 tablespoons [112 g]) unsalted butter, diced

4 oz (110 g) unbleached all-purpose flour

2 quarts (1.9 L) whole milk

½ yellow onion

1 bay leaf

1 clove

Generous pinch freshly ground nutmeg

Freshly ground black pepper

Kosher salt

Heat a small, heavy pot over medium heat until hot. Add the butter and swirl to melt and coat the bottom of the pot. When it bubbles and the foam subsides, add the flour and cook, whisking constantly, until it has a toasted aroma, about 3 minutes. Whisk in the milk, add the onion, bay leaf, clove, nutmeg, and a generous grinding of pepper. Bring to a boil, whisking constantly. Simmer, stirring frequently, until thickened and the raw, starchy flour flavor is gone, about 20 minutes. Season with salt and pepper and strain through a fine-mesh sieve. Let cool.

PASTA AND NOODLE DISHES

· · · · ·

Lasagna Bolognese

YIELDS 6 TO 8 SERVINGS

With layers of homemade lasagna, homemade ragu bolognese, homemade white sauce, and Parmigiano, this lasagna is no doubt a labor of love—but all the time and effort results in nothing less than a small miracle. This is a truly delicious, glorious dish.

Kosher salt

1 recipe fresh Egg Lasagna (pages 28 and 52)

Unsalted butter, for greasing the baking dish

¾ recipe Ragu Bolognese (page 113), chilled

½ recipe Béchamel Sauce (page 114), chilled

6 oz (170 g) freshly grated Parmigiano-Reggiano

Bring a large pot of water to a boil and salt generously.

Add two sheets of the lasagna to the boiling water and boil, stirring gently, until beginning to soften. Using a wire skimmer, remove the lasagna from the pot and transfer to a large bowl of ice water to cool as quickly as possible. Remove the lasagna from the ice water and stack between flour sack towels to dry. Boil, chill, and dry the remaining lasagna in the same manner.

Preheat the oven to 375°F (190°C, or gas mark 5).

Grease a deep 9- by 13-inch (23- by 33-cm) baking dish with the butter. Spread a generous spoonful of the ragu in the bottom of the baking dish. Arrange a layer of lasagna in the baking dish, cutting the sheets to fit as necessary. Spread with about one-sixth of the béchamel and then about one-sixth of the remaining ragu, and then sprinkle with about one-sixth of the Parmigiano. Make five more layers of lasagna, béchamel, ragu, and Parmigiano in the same manner. Cover the baking dish with foil.

To finish the dish, bake 30 minutes. Remove the foil and bake until golden brown and bubbling around the edges, about 25 minutes. Let cool for about 20 minutes before serving.

Laurie's Loaf Pan Lasagna

YIELDS 2 PANS, MAKING 4 TO 6 SERVINGS EACH

My friend Laurie, @baltimorehomecook on Instagram, is an attorney-turned-pasta-making-instructor, and I love her generous spirit and her creative yet thoughtful approach to cooking. Her signature lasagna is nothing short of brilliant. Rather than making one enormous casserole dish and winding up with leftovers for days, she uses two loaf pans, which conveniently are just the same width as pasta sheeted with a typical pasta machine. Using loaf pans means one freshly-baked lasagna now and one freshly-baked lasagna later. Or even better, it means one lasagna to eat and one lasagna to give. Laurie's known for sharing pans of her lasagna with friends and family; she says she's "sending a hug in the form of an edible gift."

Laurie's lasagna is as delicious as it is clever. It's loaded with browned meat, lots of cheese, including ricotta made from scratch and mixed with fresh pesto, and red sauce (layers that happen to be reminiscent of the Italian flag). And of course, thanks to the loaf pans, it has twice as many crunchy corners!

If eight crunchy corners still isn't enough, baked lasagna can be refrigerated in its pan and, once chilled and set, unmolded, sliced, and sautéed. Lasagna reheated in this manner will have a golden brown and crisp exterior all around.

Kosher salt

2 tablespoons (30 ml) extra-virgin olive oil

10⅔ oz (300 g) 90% lean ground beef, broken up

10⅔ oz (300 g) ground veal, broken up

10⅔ oz (300 g) ground pork, broken up

Freshly ground black pepper

1 recipe Homemade Ricotta (page 191) or store-bought, at room temperature

1 recipe Basil Pesto (page 112)

1 recipe fresh Egg Lasagna (pages 28 and 52) or other lasagna

Unsalted butter, for greasing the loaf pans

1 recipe Simple Tomato Sauce (page 108), puréed and chilled

1 lb. (455 g) mozzarella, shredded

¼ cup (12 g) minced basil

¼ cup (16 g) minced oregano

Bring a large pot of water to a boil and salt generously.

Heat a large, heavy skillet over medium-high heat until hot. Add the olive oil and swirl to coat the inside of the pan. Add about half of the meat and sear, tossing a couple of times, until golden brown all over, about 8 minutes. Remove the meat to a plate using a slotted spoon. Sear the remaining half of the meat in the same manner. Let cool to room temperature.

Transfer the beef to a food processor and pulse until minced. Season with salt and pepper.

In a bowl, blend together the ricotta and pesto.

Add two sheets of the lasagna to the boiling water and boil, stirring gently, until beginning to soften. Using a wire skimmer, remove the lasagna from the pot and transfer to a large bowl of ice water to cool as quickly as possible. Remove the lasagna from the ice water and stack between flour sack towels to dry. Boil, chill, and dry the remaining lasagna in the same manner.

Preheat the oven to 350°F (175°C, or gas mark 4).

Grease two 9¼- by 5¼- by 2¾-inch (23- by 13- by 7-cm) loaf pans with the butter. Spread a scant ladleful of the tomato sauce in the bottom of each pan. Arrange a layer of lasagna in each pan, cutting the sheets to fit as necessary. Between the two pans, spread with about one-quarter of the ricotta mixture, then sprinkle with a little less than one-quarter of the mozzarella, then about one-quarter of the meat, and then about one-quarter of the basil and oregano, and then spread with a ladleful of the tomato sauce. Make three more layers of lasagna, ricotta mixture, mozzarella, meat, basil and oregano, and tomato sauce in the same manner. Finish with a layer of the remaining tomato sauce and mozzarella in each pan and cover with foil.

To finish the dish, bake 45 minutes. Remove the foil and bake until golden brown and bubbling around the edges, about 35 minutes. Let cool for about 20 minutes before serving.

Unbaked lasagna may be kept tightly wrapped in the refrigerator for a day or two or in the freezer for several weeks. Thaw frozen lasagna in the refrigerator before baking.

Pappardelle with Sunday Pork Ragu

YIELDS 8 GENEROUS SERVINGS

If you want a satisfying, meaty tomato sauce with cooked-all-day flavor for your lovingly homemade pasta, this is definitely it. It's worth gathering the entire family around the table for this one.

1 lb. 12 oz (800 g) piece boneless pork butt

Kosher salt

Freshly ground black pepper

¼ cup (60 ml) extra-virgin olive oil

1 lb. (455 g) Homemade Bulk Spicy Italian Sausage (page 188) or store-bought, broken up

1 recipe Slow-Simmered Tomato Sauce (page 109)

⅓ cup (80 ml) red wine

2 recipes fresh Egg Pappardelle (pages 28 and 52) or other sheeted, extruded, or cavatelli maker pasta

Freshly grated Parmigiano-Reggiano, for serving

Blot the pork dry with paper towels and season generously with salt and pepper. Heat a large, heavy pot over medium-high heat until hot. Add the olive oil and swirl to coat the inside of the pot. Add the pork and sear, turning occasionally, until golden brown all over, about 12 minutes. Remove the pork to a plate. Add the sausage to the pot and fry, stirring occasionally, until golden brown, about 6 minutes. Remove the sausage to another plate. Add the tomato sauce and wine and return the pork along with any accumulated juice to the pot. Bring to a boil and simmer covered, stirring and turning the pork occasionally, for 1 hour. Return the sausage along with any accumulated juice to the pot and simmer covered, stirring and turning the pork occasionally, until the pork is fork tender, about 1 hour.

While the pork finishes cooking, bring a large pot of water to a boil and salt generously.

Remove the pork from the sauce. Shred the pork, return it to the pot, and return to a boil.

Add the pasta to the boiling water and boil, stirring frequently, until nearly al dente.

To finish the dish, season the sauce with salt and pepper. Reserve a ladleful of the pasta cooking water. Working quickly, drain the pasta, transfer it to the pot with sauce, and toss gently to coat, thinning with reserved pasta water as desired. Remove from the heat and serve immediately topped with plenty of grated Parmigiano.

Tuna Noodle Casserole

YIELDS 6 TO 8 SERVINGS

Pasta and sauce made from scratch make this the best possible version of the classic American comfort food.

If fresh peas are not available, substitute about a cup (135 g) of thawed frozen peas. There's no need to boil them along with the pasta.

Kosher salt

3 tablespoons (45 ml) extra-virgin olive oil

3 tablespoons (42 g) unsalted butter, diced, plus more for greasing the baking dish

½ yellow onion, diced

2 sprigs thyme

12 oz (335 g) button or cremini mushrooms, sliced

1 recipe fresh Egg Pappardelle (pages 28 and 52), Semolina and Oil Pappardelle (pages 35 and 52), or other sheeted or extruded pasta

1 lb. (455 g) English peas, shelled

½ recipe Béchamel Sauce (page 114), chilled

4 cans (5 oz [142 g]) water-packed tuna, drained and flaked

6 oz (170 g) shredded sharp Cheddar

¼ teaspoon Worcestershire sauce

Freshly ground black pepper

1 oz (30 g) freshly grated Parmigiano-Reggiano

Bring a large pot of water to a boil and salt generously.

Heat a large, heavy skillet over medium-low heat until hot. Add the olive oil and butter and swirl to coat the inside of the pan. When the butter bubbles and the foam subsides, add the onion and thyme. Sauté until the onion is soft, about 5 minutes. Add the mushrooms and sauté until tender, about 10 minutes. Season with salt and pepper and discard the thyme sprigs. Let cool.

Preheat the oven to 375°F (190°C, or gas mark 5).

Add the pasta and peas to the boiling water and boil, stirring frequently, until the pasta is beginning to soften and the peas are bright green. Drain the pasta and peas. With the pasta and peas still in the colander, run cold water over them while gently separating the strands to cool as quickly as possible and rinse away excess starch. Drain the pasta and peas again. Immediately combine the pasta and peas, onion and mushrooms, béchamel, tuna, Cheddar, and Worcestershire in a large bowl. Toss gently to coat. Season with salt and pepper.

Grease a deep 9- by 13-inch (23- by 33-cm) baking dish with butter. Transfer the pasta to the baking dish, spread evenly, and sprinkle with the Parmigiano. Cover the baking dish with foil.

To finish the dish, bake 30 minutes. Remove the foil and bake until golden brown and bubbling around the edges, about 25 minutes. Serve immediately.

Tagliatelle with Taleggio Sauce

YIELDS 4 GENEROUS SERVINGS

Taleggio is an Italian washed rind cow's milk cheese with a pungent aroma and mild, buttery flavor. It's great for melting. Taleggio stars along with egg pasta in this mac and cheese for adults. The sauce is creamy, a little bit sticky, and absolutely luxurious, yet it takes just minutes and almost zero effort to make.

Kosher salt

10 oz (280 g) taleggio, at room temperature

1¼ cups (295 ml) heavy cream

1 recipe fresh Egg Tagliatelle (pages 28 and 55) or other sheeted pasta

Freshly ground black pepper

2 tablespoons (6 g) minced chives

Bring a large pot of water to a boil and salt generously.

Cut the rind off the taleggio and discard. Dice the taleggio.

Bring the cream to a boil in a large, heavy skillet. Remove from the heat, add the taleggio, and cover, whisking once, until melted, about 5 minutes.

While the taleggio is melting, add the pasta to the boiling water and boil, stirring frequently, until very nearly al dente.

To finish the dish, whisk the sauce until smooth and season it with salt and pepper. Reserve a ladleful of the pasta cooking water. Working quickly, drain the pasta, transfer it to the skillet with sauce, and toss gently to coat, thinning with reserved pasta water as desired. Serve immediately topped with the chives.

Asparagus Variation: Thick, succulent spears of asparagus will cook in roughly the same time as the tagliatelle. Boil 1 bunch of asparagus, trimmed and cut into bite-size pieces, right along with the pasta.

Chocolate Tagliatelle with Pork and Red Wine Ragu

YIELDS 4 GENEROUS SERVINGS

The pairing of red wine ragu with chocolate pasta may seem strange until you try it. It is in fact a classic combination as the earthiness of wine and cocoa are surprisingly delicious together.

1 lb. 12 oz (800 g) piece boneless pork butt

Kosher salt

Freshly ground black pepper

¼ cup (60 ml) extra-virgin olive oil

1 yellow onion, diced small

2 stalks celery, diced small

1 carrot, diced small

5 cloves garlic, minced

2 tablespoons (32 g) tomato paste

2½ cups (570 ml) red wine

1 can (14½ oz [411 g]) diced tomatoes

1 bay leaf

1 sprig rosemary

1 tablespoon (4 g) minced Italian parsley

1 recipe fresh Chocolate Egg Tagliatelle (pages 32 and 55) or other sheeted pasta

Freshly grated Parmigiano-Reggiano, for serving

Blot the pork dry with paper towels and season generously with salt and pepper. Heat a large, heavy pot over medium-high heat until hot. Add the olive oil and swirl to coat the inside of the pot. Add the pork and sear, turning occasionally, until golden brown all over, about 12 minutes. Remove the pork to a plate. Lower the heat to medium-low and add the onion to the pot. Sauté until extremely soft and translucent, about 10 minutes. Add the celery and carrot and sauté until soft, about 10 minutes. Add the garlic and sauté until fragrant, about 2 minutes. Add the tomato paste and sauté until golden brown, about 3 minutes. Add the wine, tomatoes along with their liquid, bay leaf, rosemary, and parsley. Return the pork along with any accumulated juice to the pot. Bring to a boil and simmer covered, stirring and turning the pork occasionally, until the pork is fork tender, about 2 hours.

While the pork finishes cooking, bring a large pot of water to a boil and salt generously.

Remove the pork from the sauce and discard the bay leaf and rosemary sprig. Shred the pork and return it to the pot. Simmer, stirring frequently, until the sauce is thickened, about 12 minutes.

Add the pasta to the boiling water and boil, stirring frequently, until nearly al dente.

To finish the dish, season the sauce with salt and pepper. Reserve a ladleful of the pasta cooking water. Working quickly, drain the pasta, transfer it to the pot with sauce, and toss gently to coat, thinning with reserved pasta water as desired. Remove from the heat and serve immediately topped with plenty of grated Parmigiano.

Olive Variation: Add ½ cup (64 g) pitted Kalamata olives to the sauce at the same time as the wine, tomatoes, and herbs.

Tagliatelle with Crème Fraîche and Smoked Salmon

YIELDS 4 GENEROUS SERVINGS

Crème fraîche with an abundant quantity of fresh herbs makes for an instant sauce for pasta.

Kosher salt

1 recipe fresh Half Whole-Wheat Egg Tagliatelle (pages 34 and 55) or other sheeted pasta

1 cup (240 ml) Homemade Crème Fraîche (page 190) or store-bought, at room temperature

8 oz (225 g) sliced cold smoked salmon, cut into ¼-inch (6-mm)-wide strips

¼ cup (16 g) minced dill

¼ cup (12 g) minced chives

Freshly ground black pepper

Lemon wedges, for serving

Bring a large pot of water to a boil and salt generously.

Add the pasta to the boiling water and boil, stirring frequently, until very nearly al dente.

To finish the dish, reserve a ladleful of the pasta cooking water. Working quickly, drain the pasta and return it to the pot (off the heat). Add the crème fraîche, salmon, dill, and chives and toss gently to coat, thinning with reserved pasta water as desired. Season with salt and pepper. Serve immediately with the lemon wedges.

Fettuccine with Alfredo Sauce

YIELDS 4 GENEROUS SERVINGS

This extremely simple yet famous dish is all about the flavors of good egg pasta and real Parmigiano. Make it when you are in the mood for something rich, creamy, and absolutely luxurious.

It is perfect just as it is, but you can garnish it in any number of ways. If you like, toss in cooked spinach, add diced seeded Roma tomatoes, or top it with grilled chicken, cooked shrimp or crabmeat, or smoked salmon.

Kosher salt

1 cup (240 ml) heavy cream

1 stick (8 tablespoons [112 g]) unsalted butter, diced

1 clove garlic, grated using a rasp-style grater

Generous pinch freshly ground nutmeg

Freshly ground black pepper

3½ oz (100 g) freshly grated, preferably using a rasp-style grater, Parmigiano-Reggiano, plus more for serving

1 recipe fresh Egg Fettuccine (pages 28 and 55) or other sheeted pasta

Bring a large pot of water to a boil and salt generously.

Combine the cream, butter, garlic, nutmeg, and a generous grinding of pepper in a large, heavy skillet. Bring to a boil and simmer until thickened, about 5 minutes. Remove from the heat and whisk in the Parmigiano. Season with salt and pepper.

Add the pasta to the boiling water and boil, stirring frequently, until very nearly al dente.

To finish the dish, reserve a ladleful of the pasta cooking water. Working quickly, drain the pasta, transfer it to the skillet with sauce, and toss gently to coat, thinning with reserved pasta water as desired. Serve immediately topped with additional Parmigiano.

Fettuccine with Corn and Smoked Salmon

YIELDS 4 GENEROUS SERVINGS

Sweet corn is a delicious contrast to the salty richness of smoked salmon. Feel free to use more or less jalapeños to suit your taste, substitute Fresno chiles, or even use strips of roasted New Mexico green chiles in season.

Kosher salt

2 tablespoons (28 g) unsalted butter, diced

Kernels from 2 ears corn (about 2½ cups [410 g])

2 jalapeños, sliced thinly

3 tablespoons (45 ml) white wine

1 cup (240 ml) heavy cream

8–10 oz (230–280 g) hot smoked salmon, flaked

1 recipe fresh Egg Fettuccine (pages 28 and 55) or other sheeted pasta

3 green onions, sliced

Freshly ground black pepper

Freshly grated Parmigiano-Reggiano, for serving

Bring a large pot of water to a boil and salt generously.

Heat a large, heavy skillet over medium heat until hot. Add the butter and swirl to melt and coat the bottom of the pan. When it bubbles and the foam subsides, add the corn and jalapeños. Sauté until the corn turns a shade deeper, about 2 minutes. Add the wine and simmer, stirring occasionally, until nearly dry, about 2 minutes. Add the cream and bring to a boil, stirring occasionally. Add the salmon and simmer, stirring gently, until just heated through, about 2 minutes.

While the salmon is heating, add the pasta to the boiling water and boil, stirring frequently, until very nearly al dente.

To finish the dish, stir the green onions into the sauce, remove it from the heat, and season it with salt and pepper. Reserve a ladleful of the pasta cooking water. Working quickly, drain the pasta, transfer it to the skillet with sauce, and toss gently to coat, thinning with reserved pasta water as desired. Serve immediately topped with plenty of grated Parmigiano.

Chipotle Variation: Force three canned chipotles in adobo sauce through a fine-mesh sieve to remove the skins and seeds. Add the chipotle purée to the sauce at the same time as the cream.

Beef Stroganoff with Egg Noodles

YIELDS 4 GENEROUS SERVINGS

My mom makes the best beef Stroganoff ever. Her version of the Russian beef and mushrooms in a rich smetana, or sour cream, sauce is flavored with caramelized onions and slow cooked. This is her recipe, and I bet you'll love it as much as I do.

1 lb. 12 oz (800 g) piece boneless beef chuck, cut into ½- by ½- by 2-inch (1- by 1- by 5-cm) strips

Kosher salt

Freshly ground black pepper

3 tablespoons (45 ml) canola oil

1 yellow onion, julienned

8 oz (230 g) button or cremini mushrooms, sliced

¼ cup (64 g) tomato paste

1¼ cups (295 ml) Simple Beef Stock (page 196)

1 recipe fresh Egg Fettuccine (pages 28 and 55) or other sheeted pasta

½ cup (115 g) sour cream

2 tablespoons (8 g) minced Italian parsley

Season the beef generously with salt and pepper.

Heat a large, heavy skillet over medium-high heat until hot. Add the oil and swirl to coat the inside of the pot. Add half of the beef and sear, tossing a couple of times, until golden brown all over, about 7 minutes. Remove the beef to a plate using a slotted spoon. Sear the remaining beef in the same manner. Return the first batch of beef along with any accumulated juice to the skillet. Lower the heat to medium-low, add the onion and a generous pinch of salt, and sauté until the onion is light golden brown, about 45 minutes. Add the mushrooms and sauté until tender, about 10 minutes. Add the tomato paste and sauté until golden brown, about 3 minutes. Add the stock, bring to a boil, and simmer covered, stirring occasionally, until the beef is fork tender, about 2 hours.

While the beef finishes cooking, bring a large pot of water to a boil and salt generously.

Add the pasta to the boiling water and boil, stirring frequently, until very nearly al dente.

To finish the dish, remove the sauce from the heat and skim off the fat as desired. Stir in the sour cream and season with salt and pepper. Working quickly, drain the pasta and divide among individual plates. Then divide the sauce among the plates. Serve immediately topped with the parsley.

Linguine with Lemon Cream Sauce

YIELDS 4 GENEROUS SERVINGS

This combination of pasta and sauce is divine just as it is. But if you're in the mood for something really special, consider tossing in some cooked shrimp or crabmeat.

Kosher salt

1 large lemon

2 cups (475 ml) heavy cream

1 large clove garlic, grated using a rasp-style grater

1 recipe fresh All Yolk Linguine (pages 31 and 55) or other sheeted or extruded pasta

Freshly ground black pepper

Freshly grated Parmigiano-Reggiano, for serving

Bring a large pot of water to a boil and salt generously.

Zest the lemon using a rasp-style grater and cut it in half. Squeeze the juice into a medium bowl. Combine the cream, lemon zest, and garlic in a large, heavy skillet. Bring to a boil and simmer until slightly thickened, about 7 minutes.

While the cream thickens, add the pasta to the boiling water and boil, stirring frequently, until nearly al dente.

To finish the dish, stir 3 tablespoons (45 ml) of the lemon juice into the sauce. Season with salt and pepper. Reserve a ladleful of the pasta cooking water. Working quickly, drain the pasta, transfer it to the skillet with sauce, and toss gently to coat, thinning with reserved pasta water as desired. Remove from the heat and serve immediately topped with plenty of grated Parmigiano.

Chocolate Egg Fettuccine with Roasted Strawberries, Crème Fraîche, and Balsamico

YIELDS 4 GENEROUS SERVINGS

If you just can't get enough pasta for dinner, perhaps you need some for dessert? This delicious dish is actually only lightly sweetened, so it's sure to delight both sweet and savory fans at the same time. Make it during the summer when strawberries are ripe and juicy and red all the way through to the core.

1½ oz (45 g) hazelnuts

Kosher salt

1 lb. (455 g) strawberries, halved or quartered if large

3 tablespoons (39 g) sugar

3 tablespoons (45 ml) extra-virgin olive oil

½ recipe fresh Chocolate Egg Fettuccine (pages 32 and 55)

1½ oz (45 g) Homemade Cultured Butter (page 190) or store-bought, diced and cold

Freshly ground black pepper

Homemade Crème Fraîche (page 190) or store-bought, for serving

Real balsamic vinegar, for serving

Preheat the oven to 450°F (230°C, or gas mark 8). Spread the hazelnuts on a baking sheet and bake until toasted and golden brown, about 8 minutes. Let cool to room temperature. Transfer the hazelnuts to a flour sack towel, fold the towel over them, and rub to remove the skins. Transfer the hazelnuts to a cutting board and chop coarsely.

Bring a large pot of water to a boil and salt generously.

Toss together the strawberries, sugar, and olive oil in a 11- by 7-inch (28- by 18-cm) baking dish. Roast, stirring once, until the strawberries are soft and juicy, about 20 minutes.

Add the pasta to the boiling water and boil, stirring frequently, until very nearly al dente.

To finish the dish, stir the butter into the strawberries. Working quickly, drain the pasta, return it to the pot (off the heat), add the sauce, and toss gently to coat. Serve immediately topped with a grinding of pepper, the hazelnuts and crème fraîche, and a generous drizzle of balsamic vinegar.

Spaghetti alla Chitarra with Meatballs

YIELDS 4 GENEROUS SERVINGS

This is the most unfussy way to make proper spaghetti and meatballs I know. It forgoes the pan-frying in favor of roasting the meatballs, which means all of the browning with less attended cooking time and none of the greasy mess.

1 lb. 4 oz (560 g) 80% lean ground beef

1 cup (50 g) panko breadcrumbs

1¾ oz (50 g) freshly grated Parmigiano-Reggiano, plus more for serving

1 egg

3 cloves garlic, minced

1 tablespoon (16 g) tomato paste

3 tablespoons (12 g) minced Italian parsley

¼ oz (7 g) kosher salt, plus more

Freshly ground black pepper

½ recipe Slow-Simmered Tomato Sauce (page 109)

1 recipe fresh Semolina and Oil Chitarra (pages 35 and 59) or other sheeted or extruded pasta

Preheat the oven to 450°F (230°C, or gas mark 8).

Blend together the ground beef, panko, Parmigiano, egg, garlic, tomato paste, parsley, salt, and a generous grinding of pepper. Shape into 1½-inch (3.5-cm) balls. Bake the meatballs on a baking sheet until golden brown, about 16 minutes.

While the meatballs finish baking, bring the tomato sauce to a boil in a large, heavy pot. Transfer the meatballs along with any accumulated drippings to the sauce and simmer covered, stirring occasionally, until tender, about 1 hour.

While the meatballs simmer, bring a large pot of water to a boil and salt generously.

Add the pasta to the boiling water and boil, stirring frequently, until nearly al dente.

To finish the dish, season the sauce with salt and pepper. Reserve a ladleful of the pasta cooking water. Working quickly, drain the pasta, transfer it to the pot with sauce, and toss gently to coat, thinning with reserved pasta water as desired. Remove from the heat and serve immediately topped with additional Parmigiano.

Squid Ink Chitarra with Shrimp, Peas, and Pepperoni Crumbs

YIELDS 4 GENEROUS SERVINGS

The subtle briny flavor of squid ink pasta marries beautifully with shrimp and sweet peas, while rendered crunchy bits of pepperoni add irresistible savory crunch. It's the type of dish you'd expect to find on the menu of a trendy contemporary restaurant. It sounds fancy, and yet it's not at all difficult to make at home.

If you can find it, you can try substituting some sautéed 'nduja, the Calabrian spicy spreadable pork salami, for the crunchy pepperoni.

Kosher salt

3½ oz (100 g) pepperoni

2 tablespoons (30 ml) extra-virgin olive oil

4 cloves garlic, minced

½ teaspoon dried oregano

3 Roma tomatoes, diced

¼ cup (60 ml) white wine

1 lb. (455 g) 31–35 count shrimp, peeled and deveined

1 recipe fresh Squid Ink Egg Chitarra (pages 28 and 59) or other sheeted or extruded pasta

1 lb. (455 g) English peas, shelled

Freshly ground black pepper

1 tablespoon (15 ml) freshly squeezed lemon juice

Crunchy Breadcrumbs (page 194), for serving, optional

Freshly grated Parmigiano-Reggiano, for serving

Bring a large pot of water to a boil and salt generously.

Peel the casing off the pepperoni and shred it using a cheese shredder.

Heat a large, heavy skillet over medium heat until hot. Add the olive oil and swirl to coat the inside of the pan. Add the pepperoni and fry, stirring frequently, until golden brown, crisp, and rendered, about 4 minutes. Remove the pepperoni to a plate using a slotted spoon. Add the garlic and oregano to the skillet and sauté until fragrant, about 30 seconds. Add the tomatoes and cook until their juices thicken, about 3 minutes. Add the wine and shrimp and simmer until the shrimp is pink, about 3 minutes.

While the shrimp simmers, add the pasta and peas to the boiling water. Boil, stirring frequently, until nearly al dente.

To finish the dish, season the sauce with salt and pepper. Reserve a ladleful of the pasta cooking water. Working quickly, drain the pasta and peas, transfer them to the skillet with sauce, add the lemon juice and pepperoni, and toss gently to coat, thinning with reserved pasta water as desired. Remove from the heat and serve immediately topped with the Crunchy Breadcrumbs, if desired, and plenty of grated Parmigiano.

Reginette with Roasted Tomatoes

YIELDS 4 GENEROUS SERVINGS

Roasting tomatoes concentrates their flavor and brings out their sweetness. It's a nice change of pace from making stovetop pasta sauces.

Kosher salt

2 lb. (910 g) cherry tomatoes

4 cloves garlic, minced

1 tablespoon (4 g) minced oregano

1 teaspoon minced thyme

⅓ cup (80 ml) extra-virgin olive oil, plus more for serving

Freshly ground black pepper

1 recipe fresh Egg Reginette (pages 28 and 52) or other sheeted or extruded pasta

1 large handful (about ¾ oz [20 g]) basil leaves, torn if large

Freshly grated Parmigiano-Reggiano, for serving

Real balsamic vinegar, for serving

Preheat the oven to 425°F (220°C, or gas mark 6).

Bring a large pot of water to a boil and salt generously.

Toss together the tomatoes, garlic, oregano, thyme, and olive oil on a baking sheet. Season with salt and pepper. Roast until the tomatoes begin to collapse and are soft and juicy, about 25 minutes.

Add the pasta to the boiling water and boil, stirring frequently, until very nearly al dente.

To finish the dish, reserve a ladleful of the pasta cooking water. Working quickly, drain the pasta, return it to the pot (off the heat), and add the sauce and basil. Toss gently to coat, thinning with reserved pasta water as desired. Serve immediately topped with plenty of grated Parmigiano and a drizzle of balsamic vinegar.

Corn Variation: Toss kernels from 1 or 2 large ears corn with the tomatoes before roasting. Serve with Corn Egg Reginette (pages 32 and 52).

Quadrucci with Melted Zucchini

YIELDS 4 GENEROUS SERVINGS

This recipe is great in the summer, when there is an abundance of young, tender zucchini at the market. It breaks all the normal cooking rules—you overcrowd the pot to start and then let the zucchini stew in its own juices for a while. What seems to be a giant pile of zucchini will eventually "melt," or cook down, into a thick sauce.

The kid in me loves the texture of this dish with pastina, or small pasta cuts which are usually used for soup. I actually make it with orzo when I'm too pressed for time to make pasta from scratch, but it would be good with most any type or shape of pasta.

¼ cup (60 ml) plus 2 tablespoons (30 ml) extra-virgin olive oil, divided

3 lb. 5 oz (1500 g) zucchini, diced into ¼-inch (6-mm) cubes

Kosher salt

6 cloves garlic, minced

1 teaspoon dried basil

1 teaspoon dried oregano

Generous pinch red chile flakes

Freshly ground black pepper

1 recipe fresh Semolina and Oil Quadrucci (pages 35 and 55) or other sheeted, extruded, or cavatelli maker pasta

4 tablespoons (55 g or ½ stick) unsalted butter, diced

Freshly grated Parmigiano-Reggiano, for serving

Heat a large, heavy pot over medium heat until hot. Add ¼ cup (60 ml) of the olive oil and swirl to coat the inside of the pot. Add the zucchini and a couple of generous pinches of salt and cook, stirring frequently, until extremely soft and translucent and beginning to brown on the bottom, about 35 minutes.

While the zucchini is cooking, bring a large pot of water to a boil and salt generously.

Nudge the zucchini to the sides of the pot, add the remaining olive oil to the center of the pot, and add the garlic, basil, oregano, chile flakes, and a generous grinding of pepper. Sauté until the garlic is fragrant, about 2 minutes. Stir the garlic and herbs into the zucchini and continue to cook, stirring frequently, until all the zucchini is "melted," about 6 minutes.

While the zucchini finishes cooking, add the pasta to the boiling water and boil, stirring frequently, until nearly al dente.

To finish the dish, season the sauce with salt and pepper. Reserve a ladleful of the pasta cooking water. Working quickly, drain the pasta, transfer it to the pot with the sauce, and toss gently to coat, thinning with reserved pasta water as desired. Remove from the heat, stir in the butter, and serve immediately topped with plenty of grated Parmigiano.

Turkey Meatball Soup with Pasta and Vegetables

YIELDS 4 GENEROUS SERVINGS

Loaded with tender meatballs, vibrant veggies, and pastina, this soup is simple, satisfying, and healthy. It's certain to make it into your regular dinner rotation.

1 lb. (455 g) ground turkey

¾ cup (38 g) panko breadcrumbs

1¼ oz (35 g) freshly grated Parmigiano-Reggiano, plus more for serving

1 egg

3 cloves garlic, minced

1 tablespoon (3 g) minced sage

1½ teaspoons (6 g) kosher salt, plus more for seasoning

Freshly ground black pepper

2 quarts (1.9 L) Simple Chicken Stock (page 195)

1 can (14½ oz [411 g]) diced tomatoes

2 stalks celery, sliced

1 carrot, sliced

½ recipe fresh Rye Egg Quadrucci (pages 34 and 55) or other sheeted or extruded pasta

6 oz (170 g) baby spinach

Blend together the ground turkey, panko, Parmigiano, egg, garlic, sage, salt, and a generous grinding of pepper. Shape into 1-inch (2.5-cm) balls.

Combine the stock and tomatoes along with their liquid in a large, heavy pot. Bring to a boil. Add the meatballs, celery, and carrot. Return to a boil, and simmer until the meatballs are just cooked through, about 4 minutes. Add the pasta and a generous pinch of salt and simmer, stirring frequently, until nearly al dente. Add the spinach and stir until it's wilted, about 1 minute. Season with salt and pepper and serve immediately topped with plenty of grated Parmigiano.

Farfalle with Roast Cauliflower, Caper, and Brown Butter Sauce

YIELDS 4 GENEROUS SERVINGS

There is no better way to coax flavor out of a head of cauliflower than to roast it whole at a high temperature. Basted with butter, it becomes a dark mahogany brown, with flesh that yields to the gentlest pressure, a seductive silky texture, and a depth of flavor that's both nutty and sweet. With plenty of capers, shallots, and anchovies, it becomes a delicious sauce for any type of pasta but especially for Half Whole-Wheat Egg Farfalle.

1 large (about 2 lb. [910 g]) head cauliflower

¼ cup (60 ml) extra-virgin olive oil

1 stick (8 tablespoons [112 g]) unsalted butter, diced

Kosher salt

3 tablespoons (27 g) capers

1 large shallot, diced

2 anchovy fillets, minced

Generous pinch red chile flakes

1 recipe fresh Half Whole-Wheat Egg Farfalle (pages 34 and 56) or other sheeted or extruded pasta

¼ cup (15 g) minced Italian parsley

Freshly ground black pepper

Crunchy Breadcrumbs (page 194), for serving, optional

Freshly grated Parmigiano-Reggiano, for serving

Preheat the oven to 450°F (230°C, or gas mark 8).

Add the cauliflower to a large, heavy skillet. Drizzle with the olive oil, and roast for 30 minutes. Add the butter to the skillet and continue to roast, basting every 15 minutes, until the cauliflower is deeply browned and a paring knife inserted into the center meets no resistance, about 1 hour more.

While the cauliflower is roasting, bring a large pot of water to a boil and salt generously.

Transfer the skillet to the stovetop over medium-low heat, nudge the cauliflower to the side of the skillet, and add the capers, shallot, anchovies, and chile flakes to the brown butter. Sauté until the shallot is soft, about 2 minutes.

While the capers and shallot are sautéeing, add the pasta to the boiling water and boil, stirring frequently, until nearly al dente.

To finish the dish, break up the cauliflower into bite-size pieces and toss it with the sauce. Stir in the parsley and season with salt and pepper. Reserve a ladleful of the pasta cooking water. Working quickly, drain the pasta, transfer it to the skillet with sauce, add ⅓ cup (80 ml) of the reserved pasta water, and toss gently to coat, thinning with additional pasta water as desired. Remove from the heat and serve immediately topped with the Crunchy Breadcrumbs, if desired, and plenty of grated Parmigiano.

Corzetti with Pesto, Potatoes, and Green Beans

YIELDS 4 GENEROUS SERVINGS

It may seem odd to pair pasta and potatoes together, but in this classic Ligurian dish, the starch of the potatoes gives the sauce an extra creaminess.

The recipe's quite easy to throw together because all of the ingredients are boiled together right in the same pot. The only trick is getting the timing right so that everything's done at the same moment. Just test for doneness often and use your best judgment on when the potatoes and green beans seem to be about 3 or 4 minutes away from being done to add the pasta.

2 medium (about 1 lb. [455 g]) Yukon Gold potatoes, cut into scant ¼-inch (6-mm)-thick slices

Kosher salt

12 oz (340 g) green beans, cut into bite-size pieces

¾ recipe fresh Egg Corzetti (pages 28 and 59), Half Semolina Egg Corzetti (pages 35 and 59), or All-Purpose Noodle Corzetti (pages 35 and 59) or other sheeted or extruded pasta

1 recipe Basil Pesto (page 112)

Freshly grated Parmigiano-Reggiano, for serving

Bring a large pot of water with the potatoes to a boil and salt generously. Add the green beans as soon as the water starts steaming and bubbles start breaking the surface and simmer, stirring occasionally, until the potatoes are green beans are nearly tender, about 12 minutes. Add the pasta and boil, stirring frequently, until the pasta is very nearly al dente and the potatoes and green beans are tender.

To finish the dish, reserve a ladleful of the pasta cooking water. Working quickly, drain the pasta, potatoes, and green beans, and return them to the pot (off the heat). Add the pesto and toss gently to coat, thinning with reserved pasta water as desired. Serve immediately topped with plenty of grated Parmigiano.

Garganelli with Peas and Prosciutto

YIELDS 4 GENEROUS SERVINGS

The combination of salty prosciutto and Parmigiano and sweet fresh peas is a classic.
If you don't feel like splurging on prosciutto, any good-quality ham could be substituted.

Kosher salt

1 cup (240 ml) heavy cream

1 large clove garlic, grated using
a rasp-style grater

Generous pinch saffron

Freshly ground black pepper

3 oz (85 g) freshly grated,
preferably using a rasp-style grater,
Parmigiano-Reggiano, plus more
for serving

1 recipe fresh Egg Garganelli
(pages 28 and 59) or other
sheeted pasta

1½ lb. (670 g) English peas, shelled

5⅓–8 oz (150–225 g) sliced
prosciutto, cut into ¼-inch (6-mm)-
wide strips and separated

Bring a large pot of water to a boil and salt generously.

Combine the cream, garlic, saffron, and a generous grinding of pepper in
a large, heavy skillet. Bring to a boil and simmer until slightly thickened,
about 2 minutes. Remove from the heat and whisk in the Parmigiano.
Season with salt and pepper.

Add the pasta and peas to the boiling water and boil, stirring frequently,
until the pasta is very nearly al dente and the peas are tender.

To finish the dish, reserve a ladleful of the pasta cooking water. Working
quickly, drain the pasta and peas, transfer them to the skillet with sauce.
Toss gently to coat, sprinkling in the prosciutto and thinning with
reserved pasta water as desired. Serve immediately topped with
additional Parmigiano.

Pasta Primavera with Artichoke Hearts, Asparagus, Fava Beans, Peas, and Morels

YIELDS 4 GENEROUS SERVINGS

This light pasta, with plenty of lemon and fresh herbs, showcases the beautiful produce of spring. While the preparation of fresh artichokes, fava beans, and morels requires a small investment of time, thick, succulent spears of asparagus and English peas are boiled right along with the pasta as they have roughly the same cooking time. The artichoke poaching liquid can be reused for shrimp or fish fillets.

2 large lemons

2 cloves garlic, smashed

¼ cup (60 ml) plus 1 tablespoon (15 ml) extra-virgin olive oil, divided, plus more for serving

1 bay leaf

Generous pinch red chile flakes

Kosher salt

4 medium artichokes

1 lb. (455 g) fava beans, shelled

3½ oz (100 g) morels, cut into bite-size pieces

1 recipe fresh Egg Garganelli (pages 28 and 59), Egg Tagliatelle (pages 28 and 55), or other sheeted or extruded pasta

8 oz (230 g) English peas, shelled

1 lb. (455 g) asparagus, trimmed and cut into bite-size pieces

Freshly ground black pepper

2 tablespoons (6 g) minced chives

2 tablespoons (8 g) minced Italian parsley

1 tablespoon (6 g) minced mint

1 tablespoon (6 g) minced chervil

Freshly grated Parmigiano-Reggiano, for serving

Slice 1 of the lemons. Combine 2 quarts (1.9 liters) of water, the lemon slices, garlic, 1 tablespoon (15 ml) of the olive oil, bay leaf, chile flakes, and a generous pinch of salt in a small, heavy pot. Bring to a boil and simmer until fragrant, about 15 minutes. Meanwhile, zest the remaining lemon using a rasp-style grater and cut it in half. Squeeze the juice of half of the lemon into a medium bowl of cold water. Prepare the artichoke hearts by trimming away all of the petals using a paring knife and scooping out the fuzzy choke using a melon baller. Add the artichoke hearts to the bowl of lemon water as they are trimmed to prevent oxidation. Drain the artichoke hearts, transfer them to the poaching liquid, and simmer until tender, about 25 minutes.

While the artichoke hearts cook, bring a small pot of water to a boil and salt generously. Add the favas and boil until tender, about 2 minutes. Drain the favas and transfer to a large bowl of ice water to cool as quickly as possible. Drain the favas again and then skin them.

Using a wire skimmer, remove the artichoke hearts from the poaching liquid to a cutting board, let cool, and cut into bite-size pieces.

Bring a large pot of water to a boil and salt generously.

(continued)

Heat a large, heavy skillet over medium heat until hot. Add 3 tablespoons (45 ml) of the olive oil and swirl to coat the inside of the pan. Add the morels and sauté until tender, about 4 minutes. Add the artichoke hearts and favas. Sauté until heated through and slightly browned, about 3 minutes.

While the morels, artichoke hearts, and favas cook, add the pasta, peas, and asparagus to the boiling water and boil, stirring frequently, until the pasta is nearly al dente and the peas and asparagus are tender.

To finish the dish, season the morels, artichokes, and fava beans with salt and pepper. Reserve a ladleful of the pasta cooking water. Working quickly, drain the pasta, peas, and asparagus, transfer them to the pot with sauce. Add the chives, parsley, mint, chervil, remaining 1 tablespoon (15 ml) of olive oil, and lemon zest, and squeeze over the juice of the remaining half of the lemon. Toss gently to coat, thinning with reserved pasta water as desired. Remove from the heat and serve immediately topped with a generous drizzle of olive oil and plenty of grated Parmigiano.

Taiwanese Beef Noodle Soup

YIELDS 4 TO 6 SERVINGS

This rich, aromatic, and slightly spicy soup is considered the national dish of Taiwan. It's chock-full of bok choy, meltingly tender braised beef, and slurpable noodles.

Look for Tien Tsin chiles, doubanjiang, also known as fermented chile bean paste, Shaoxing rice wine, dark soy sauce, which is used for color, dried tangerine peel, and Szechuan peppercorns, at your local Chinese market.

---

3 lb. 4 oz (905 g) meaty beef shanks, 1½-inch (3.5-cm)-thick slices

Kosher salt

2 tablespoons (30 ml) canola oil

4 cloves garlic, crushed lightly

¾ oz (20 g) ginger, cut into 3 slices and crushed lightly

4 green onions, green parts sliced

4 Tien Tsin chiles

1 tablespoon (22 g) doubanjiang

1 Roma tomato, diced small

2 tablespoons (30 ml) Shaoxing rice wine

2 quarts (1.9 L) Simple Beef Stock (page 196)

3 tablespoons (45 ml) soy sauce

1 teaspoon dark soy sauce

1 tablespoon (15 ml) sugar

1 piece (about 1-inch [2.5-cm]) dried tangerine peel

1 star anise

1 small cinnamon stick

1 bay leaf

1 teaspoon Szechuan peppercorns

¼ teaspoon fennel seeds

1 clove

Freshly ground black pepper

1 lb. 4 oz (565 g) baby bok choy, quartered

1 recipe fresh All-Purpose Noodles (pages 35 and 59)

Chopped cilantro, for serving

Blot the beef shanks dry with paper towels and season generously with salt. Heat a large, heavy pot over medium-high heat until hot. Add the canola oil and swirl to coat the inside of the pot. Add half of the shanks and sear, turning once, until golden brown all over, about 7 minutes. Remove the shanks to a plate. Sear the remaining shanks in the same manner. Add the garlic, ginger, and white parts of the green onion to the pot and sauté until golden brown, about 1 minute. Add the chiles and sauté until golden brown, about 30 seconds. Remove the garlic, ginger, green onion ends, and chiles to a plate. Lower the heat to medium-low, add the doubanjiang to the pot and sauté until aromatic, about 30 seconds. Add the tomatoes and cook until their juices thicken, about 2 minutes. Add the rice wine and simmer until nearly dry, about 1 minute. Add the stock, soy sauce, dark soy sauce, and sugar. Return the shanks along with any accumulated juice to the pot.

Combine the tangerine peel, star anise, cinnamon stick, bay leaf, Szechuan peppercorns, fennel seeds, clove, and the sautéed garlic, ginger, green onion ends, and chiles in a spice bag and cinch shut. Add the spice bag to the pot, bring to a boil, and simmer covered, skimming off any foam that rises to the surface and stirring and turning the shanks occasionally, until the beef is fork tender, about 3 hours.

While the shanks finish cooking, bring a large pot of water to a boil and salt generously.

Discard the spice bag. Remove the shanks to a plate and let cool.

While the shanks cool, skim the fat off the broth as desired. Season with salt and pepper.

When the beef is cool enough to handle, remove the meat from the bone and shred coarsely.

To finish the dish, return the broth to a boil. Add the bok choy to the boiling water and boil until tender, about 4 minutes. Using a wire skimmer, remove the bok choy from the boiling water. Return the water to a boil. Add the noodles and boil, stirring frequently, until nearly tender. Working quickly, drain the noodles and divide among individual noodle bowls. Then divide the bok choy and shredded beef and then the broth among the bowls. Serve immediately topped with the cilantro and sliced green onions.

Pork Belly Noodle Bowls with Szechuan Chile Oil

YIELDS 4 TO 6 SERVINGS

This recipe may have a long list of ingredients, but it is extremely simple to make and requires little preparation time. You don't even have to mince the ginger or garlic. In fact it's so easy, it's hard to believe how insanely delicious and satisfying it is. The braised pork belly cooks up meltingly tender and moist and, along with baby bok choy and homemade chile oil, is just the ideal topping for a bowl of wide, slippery noodles.

Look for Szechuan chile powder, Chinese black cardamom, which has a smoky slightly medicinal character, Szechuan peppercorns, Tien Tsin chiles, dark soy sauce which is used for color, Shaoxing rice wine, and Chinkiang vinegar, also known as Chinese black vinegar, at your local Chinese market.

3 tablespoons (9 g) coarse Szechuan chile powder

Kosher salt

2 Chinese black cardamom pods, divided

2 star anise, divided

2 small cinnamon sticks, divided

2 bay leaves, divided

2 teaspoons (5 g) Szechuan peppercorns, divided

2 cloves garlic, sliced thinly, plus 3 cloves, crushed lightly

¼ oz (7 g) ginger, sliced thinly, plus ¾ oz (20 g), cut into 3 slices and crushed lightly

¼ cup (60 ml) canola oil

4 Tien Tsin chiles

1 lb. 10 oz (740 g) piece boneless, skin-on pork belly, cut into 1½-inch (3.5-cm) pieces

2 tablespoons (30 ml) soy sauce, plus more for serving

1 teaspoon dark soy sauce

1 tablespoon (15 ml) Shaoxing rice wine

1 tablespoon (15 ml) Chinkiang vinegar, plus more for serving

2 tablespoons (26 g) sugar

1 lb. 4 oz (565 g) baby bok choy, quartered

1 recipe fresh All-Purpose Noodles (pages 35 and 59) or Green Tea Noodles (pages 37 and 59)

Chopped cilantro, for serving

Sliced green onions, for serving

Combine the chile powder and a generous pinch salt in a medium heat-proof bowl. Combine one of the cardamom pods, star anise, cinnamon stick, and bay leaf, 1 teaspoon of the Szechuan peppercorns, sliced garlic, the thinly sliced ginger, and canola oil in a small, heavy saucepan. Heat over medium heat, stirring occasionally, until the garlic is light golden brown, about 4 minutes. Carefully pour the hot oil through a fine-mesh sieve over the chile powder. It will bubble up dramatically. Stir the oil and chile powder until the bubbling subsides. Let cool to room temperature.

Meanwhile, combine remaining cardamom pod, star anise, cinnamon stick, bay leaf, Szechuan peppercorns, crushed garlic, crushed sliced ginger, and chiles in a spice bag and cinch shut. Combine the pork belly, soy sauce, dark soy sauce, rice wine, Chinkiang vinegar, sugar, and 2½ cups (570 ml) of water in a wok. Add the spice bag. Bring to a boil and simmer covered, stirring and turning the pork occasionally, until the pork is fork tender, about 1 hour. Discard the spice bag and simmer, stirring frequently, until the sauce is thickened, about 18 minutes.

While the sauce thickens, bring a large pot of water to a boil and salt generously.

To finish the dish, add the bok choy to the boiling water and boil until tender, about 4 minutes. Using a wire skimmer, remove the bok choy from the boiling water. Return the water to a boil. Add the noodles and boil, stirring frequently, until just tender. Working quickly, drain the noodles and divide among individual noodle bowls. Then divide the bok choy and pork belly and its sauce among the bowls. Serve immediately topped with the chile oil, cilantro, green onions, and a drizzle of soy sauce and Chinkiang vinegar.

Chicken Noodle Soup

YIELDS 4 TO 6 SERVINGS

Rich and hearty, this version of the American comfort food classic is absolutely loaded with noodles and moist, succulent shredded chicken.

Cooking the noodles separately rather than directly in the broth keeps the soup from becoming overly thick and cloudy from the dusting flour.

1 recipe Simple Chicken Stock (page 195)

8 (about 2 lb. 4 oz [1 kg]) chicken drumsticks

1 bay leaf

3 sprigs thyme

4 stalks celery, sliced thickly

2 carrots, sliced thickly

Kosher salt

Freshly ground black pepper

1 recipe fresh All-Purpose Noodles (pages 35 and 59), Whey Noodles (pages 37 and 59), Sourdough Noodles (pages 37 and 59), or other sheeted pasta

2 tablespoons (8 g) minced Italian parsley, optional

Combine the stock, chicken drumsticks, bay leaf, and thyme in a large, heavy pot. Bring to a boil and simmer slowly until the drumsticks are cooked through and the meat pulls away from the joints, about 25 minutes. Remove the chicken to a plate and let cool.

While the chicken cools, add the celery and carrots to the stock, and simmer slowly until tender, about 30 minutes.

While the celery and carrots cook, bring a large pot of water to a boil and salt generously.

When the chicken is cool enough to handle, remove the meat from the bone and shred, discarding the skin, if desired. Return the meat along with any accumulated juice to the pot. Return to a boil and reduce to a simmer.

To finish the dish, season the soup with salt and pepper. Discard the bay leaf and thyme sprigs. Add the noodles to the boiling water and boil, stirring frequently, until nearly tender. Drain the noodles, transfer them to the soup, and stir gently to combine. Remove from the heat and serve immediately topped with parsley, if desired.

Chicken Lo Mein

YIELDS 2 TO 3 SERVINGS

This take on the Chinese restaurant standard has crunchy vegetables, succulent chicken, chewy noodles, and most importantly wok hei, or the flavor of the wok.

For stir-frying, sheet noodle dough relatively thick—I use setting number 3 on my KitchenAid sheeter attachment—and cut into ⅛-inch (3-mm) wide noodles.

If you'd like to serve the whole family, quickly stir-fry two batches back to back. Simply doubling the recipe would overcrowd the wok.

Kosher salt

12 oz (340 g) boneless, skinless chicken thighs, cut into cut into ½- by ½- by 2-inch (1- by 1- by 5-cm) strips

¼ cup (60 ml) soy sauce, divided

1 tablespoon (15 ml) oyster sauce

½ teaspoon sugar

½ recipe fresh All-Purpose Noodles (pages 35 and 59), Green Tea Noodles (pages 37 and 59), Udon (page 38), or Ramen (page 38)

¼ cup (60 ml) plus 1 tablespoon (15 ml) canola oil, divided

¼ medium (about 6 oz [170 g]) cabbage, shredded

1 carrot, julienned

4 oz (110 g) mung bean sprouts

3 large cloves garlic, minced

6 green onions, cut into 1-inch (2.5-cm) pieces

Bring a large pot of water to a boil and salt generously.

Mix together the chicken, 1 tablespoon (15 ml) of the soy sauce, oyster sauce, and sugar.

Add the noodles to the boiling water and boil, stirring frequently until beginning to soften. Working quickly, drain the noodles. With the noodles still in the colander, run cold water over them while gently separating the strands to cool as quickly as possible and rinse away excess starch. Drain the noodles thoroughly and toss gently with 1 tablespoon (15 ml) of the canola oil to coat.

To finish the dish, heat a large wok over high heat until hot and beginning to smoke. Add 1 tablespoon (15 ml) of the oil and swirl to coat the inside of the wok. Add the chicken and stir-fry until golden brown but not necessarily cooked through, about 3 minutes. Remove the chicken to a bowl. Add 1 tablespoon (15 ml) of the oil to the wok and swirl to coat the inside of the wok. Add the cabbage and stir-fry until beginning to soften, about 1 minute. Add the carrot and stir-fry until beginning to soften, about 1 minute. Add the bean sprouts and stir-fry until beginning to soften, about 1 minute. Remove the vegetables to the bowl with the chicken. Add the remaining 2 tablespoons (30 ml) of oil to the wok and swirl to coat. Add the noodles and stir-fry until golden brown in spots, about 1 minute. Nudge the noodles to the sides of the wok, add the garlic to the center of the wok and stir-fry until fragrant, about 15 seconds. Toss the garlic into the noodles. Return the chicken and vegetables to the wok, add the green onions and remaining 3 tablespoons (45 ml) soy sauce, and stir-fry until heated through, about 2 minutes. Serve immediately.

Wonton Soup

YIELDS 4 TO 6 SERVINGS

Takeout pales in comparison to this soup, which is overflowing with delicious wontons and substantial enough to be served as a main course.

3 quarts (2.8 L) Simple Chicken Stock (page 195)

¼ cup (60 ml) soy sauce

2 cloves garlic, grated using a fine rasp-style grater

1 teaspoon ginger, grated using a rasp-style grater

Freshly ground white pepper

½ medium (about 14 oz [400 g]) Napa cabbage, cut into large bite-size pieces

1 recipe Pork and Shrimp Wontons (pages 67 and 73)

½ teaspoon toasted sesame oil

Sliced green onions, for serving

Combine the chicken stock, soy sauce, garlic, ginger, and a generous grinding of white pepper in a large, heavy pot. Bring to a boil. Add the Napa and simmer, stirring occasionally, until tender, about 4 minutes. Add the wontons, return to a boil, and boil, stirring frequently, until the wontons skins are just tender. Stir in the sesame oil and serve immediately topped with the green onions.

Fried Wontons
with Soy Dipping Sauce

YIELDS 4 TO 6 SERVINGS

Pork and Shrimp Wontons can be deep-fried as well as boiled for a tremendous appetizer
or snack.

1½ quarts (1.4 L) canola oil

3 tablespoons (45 ml) soy sauce

1 tablespoon (15 ml) rice vinegar

¾ teaspoon toasted sesame oil

1 jalapeño, sliced

36 Pork and Shrimp Wontons
(pages 67 and 71)

Heat the canola oil in a large, heavy pot to 365°F (185°C).

While the oil heats, mix together the soy sauce, rice vinegar, sesame oil,
and jalapeño.

To finish the dish, add 12 of the wontons to the hot oil and deep-fry
until golden brown, about 2 minutes. Using a wire skimmer, remove the
wontons to a paper towel–lined sheet tray and let drain. Reheat the oil and
fry the remaining wontons in 2 more batches in the same manner. Serve
the wontons immediately with the dipping sauce on the side.

Shoyu Ramen

YIELDS 4 GENEROUS SERVINGS

Here's a ramen noodle soup recipe that isn't too daunting to undertake at home. It has all the fixings, including a streamlined soy-flavored broth, generous portions of roast pork belly, and soft-cooked eggs. The trickiest part is peeling the delicate eggs so that they don't break.

To make Chinese five-spice, simply grind equal amounts of cinnamon, cloves, fennel seeds, star anise, and Szechuan peppercorns together in a spice mill. Sake rice wine—the sweetened cooking wine known as mirin—prepared Chinese five-spice, kombu, or dried kelp, menma, which is fermented bamboo shoots, and nori seaweed are all available at Asian markets.

¼ cup (60 ml) plus 2 tablespoons (30 ml) soy sauce, divided

1 tablespoon (15 ml) sake

2 tablespoons (30 ml) mirin, divided

2 large cloves garlic, grated using a fine rasp-style grater, divided

¼ teaspoon Chinese five-spice

2 lb. (905 g) skinless pork belly

4 eggs, at room temperature

Kosher salt

5 oz (140 g) baby spinach

2 quarts (1.9 L) Simple Chicken Stock (page 195)

1 square (4-inch [10-cm]) kombu

1 recipe fresh Ramen (page 38)

½ teaspoon toasted sesame oil

4 oz (110 g) menma

Sliced green onions, for serving

Julienned nori, for serving

Mix together 2 tablespoons (30 ml) of the soy sauce, sake, 1 tablespoon (15 ml) of the mirin, half of the grated garlic, and Chinese five-spice in a 1-gallon (3.8-liter) zip-top bag. Add the pork belly and turn to coat. Seal the bag, letting out all the air. Marinate 4 to 6 hours in the refrigerator.

Preheat the oven to 250°F (120°C, or gas mark ½).

Transfer the pork belly fat side up to a rack on a baking sheet and roast until a meat thermometer registers 180°F (82°C) when inserted into the thickest part, about 4 hours, for fork tender yet sliceable. Roast until 190°F (88°C) for unctuous and meltingly tender but more difficult to slice as it tends to shred.

While the pork belly roasts, bring a small pot of water to a boil.

Gently lower the eggs into the boiling water and simmer slowly for 6 minutes for soft-cooked. Using a wire skimmer, remove the eggs from the pot and transfer to a large bowl of ice water to cool as quickly as possible. Salt the boiling water generously, add the spinach, and boil until wilted, about 30 seconds. Drain the spinach and transfer to a large bowl of ice water to cool as quickly as possible. Drain the spinach thoroughly. When the eggs are ice cold, tap them all over with the back of a spoon to crack the shells and then peel carefully.

Transfer the pork belly to a cutting board and let rest for about 20 minutes.

While the pork belly rests, bring a large pot of water to a boil and salt generously. Combine the chicken stock, kombu, and the remaining soy sauce, mirin, and garlic in a small, heavy pot. Bring to a boil.

Carve the pork belly against the grain into thick slices and then cut the slices in half.

Add the ramen to the boiling water and boil, stirring frequently, until nearly tender.

To finish the dish, stir the sesame oil into the soup and discard the kombu. Working quickly, drain the noodles and divide among individual noodle bowls. Then divide the pork belly, spinach, and menma and then the broth among the bowls. Halve the eggs using a cheese wire and arrange cut-side up atop the noodles. Serve immediately topped with the green onions and nori.

Zaru Soba

YIELDS 4 GENEROUS SERVINGS

This Japanese dish of chilled soba with an umami-rich dipping sauce is welcome on a hot day.

Kombu, or dried kelp; the sweetened cooking wine known as mirin; katsuobushi, which is also called bonito flakes; and nori seaweed are all available at Asian markets and in the international section of most well-stocked grocers.

1 square (3-inch [7.5-cm]) kombu

⅓ cup (80 ml) soy sauce

3 tablespoons (45 ml) mirin

2 tablespoons (30 ml) rice vinegar

⅒ oz (3 g) katsuobushi

Kosher salt

1 recipe fresh Soba (page 39)

Sliced green onions, for serving

Toasted sesame seeds, for serving

Julienned nori, for serving

Grated fresh wasabi or wasabi paste, for serving

Combine the kombu and 1½ cups (355 ml) of water in a small, heavy saucepan and soak until hydrated, about 2 hours.

Add the soy sauce, mirin, and rice vinegar to the saucepan with the kombu and bring to a boil. Remove from the heat, discard the kombu, and add the katsuobushi. Strain through a fine-mesh sieve when the katsuobushi sinks to the bottom of the pan. Let cool to room temperature.

Bring a large pot of water to a boil and salt generously. Add the soba and boil, stirring frequently, until very nearly tender. Working quickly, drain the soba. With the soba still in the colander, run cold water over it while gently separating the strands to cool as quickly as possible and rinse away excess starch. Drain the soba thoroughly.

To finish the dish, divide the sauce among individual dipping bowls. Divide the soba among individual plates. Serve immediately topped with the green onions, sesame seeds, and nori and with the dipping sauce and wasabi on the side.

Miso Soup with Shrimp and Udon

YIELDS 4 GENEROUS SERVINGS

This delicious soup, which includes homemade dashi, the foundational stock of Japanese cuisine, shiitake mushrooms, miso, and nori, is light, healthy, and high in umami.

Aside from water, the two main ingredients of dashi are kombu, or dried kelp, and katsuobushi, which is also called bonito flakes. They are available at Asian markets and in the international section of most well-stocked grocers, as are miso fermented soybean paste and nori seaweed.

1 square (6-inch [15-cm]) kombu

Kosher salt

4 dried shiitake mushrooms

½ oz (14 g) katsuobushi

2 tablespoons (16 g) toasted sesame seeds

1 recipe fresh Udon (page 38)

8 oz (225 g) 16–20 count shrimp, peeled and deveined

¼ cup (64 g) red miso

Sliced green onions, for serving

Julienned nori, for serving

Combine the kombu and 2 quarts (1.9 liters) of water in a small, heavy pot. Soak until hydrated, about 2 hours.

Bring a large pot of water to a boil and salt generously.

Bring the kombu broth to a boil.

Combine the shiitakes and just enough of the hot kombu broth to cover in a medium bowl. Let soak until rehydrated and pliable, about 15 minutes. Grind the sesame seeds coarsely with mortar and pestle.

Remove the kombu broth from the heat, discard the kombu, and add the katsuobushi. Strain and reserve broth through a fine-mesh sieve when the katsuobushi sinks to the bottom of the pot. Return the dashi to the pot and return to a boil.

While the dashi heats, transfer the shiitakes to a cutting board, trim off and discard the stems, and slice the caps. Add to the dashi. Strain the shiitake soaking liquid into the dashi.

Add the udon to the boiling water and boil, stirring frequently, until nearly tender.

While the udon cooks, add the shrimp to the dashi and cook until the shrimp is pink, about 3 minutes. Meanwhile, combine the miso and a ladleful of the dashi in a medium bowl and stir until smooth. Remove the soup from the heat and stir in the miso.

To finish the dish, working quickly, drain the noodles and divide among individual noodle bowls. Then divide the soup among the bowls. Serve immediately topped with the crushed sesame seeds, green onions, and nori.

Aglio e Olio

YIELDS 4 GENEROUS SERVINGS

"Garlic and Oil" is the perhaps the simplest and most basic of all sauces, with the exception of good old butter and cheese. It is a classic pantry sauce, ready in just the time it takes to cook the pasta. Typically, it's made with store-bought dry pasta, but its simplicity allows the flavor and texture of homemade fresh pasta to shine bright.

Starting garlic slices in cold oil results in a mellow, sweet flavor similar to that of roasted garlic.

I make this dish all the time and riff on it endlessly. Depending on my mood, I might mince the garlic and start it in hot oil for a more pungent flavor. I might use Calabrian or Controne chile, piment d'espelette, or even fresh thinly sliced Fresno chiles. Sometimes I toss some broccoli florets in along with the pasta as its boiling. Often, I top it with fresh mozzarella pearls or crumbled sharp feta.

Kosher salt

¼ cup (60 ml) extra-virgin olive oil, plus more for serving

4 large cloves garlic, sliced thinly

1 recipe fresh Semolina Spaghetti (pages 78 and 85) or other sheeted, extruded, or cavatelli maker pasta

Several generous pinches red chile flakes

Freshly ground black pepper

3 tablespoons (12 g) minced Italian parsley

Freshly grated Parmigiano-Reggiano, for serving

Bring a large pot of water to a boil and salt generously.

Combine the olive oil and garlic in a large, heavy skillet. Heat over medium heat, stirring occasionally, until the garlic is light golden brown, about 4 minutes.

While the garlic is toasting, add the pasta to the boiling water and boil, stirring frequently, until nearly al dente.

To finish the dish, stir the chile flakes and a generous grinding of pepper into the skillet with the garlic. Stir in the parsley and season the sauce with salt. Reserve a ladleful of the pasta cooking water. Working quickly, drain the pasta, transfer it to the skillet with sauce, add ¼ cup (60 ml) of the reserved pasta water, and toss gently to coat, thinning with additional pasta water as desired. Remove from the heat and serve immediately topped with a generous drizzle of olive oil and plenty of grated Parmigiano.

Bucatini Carbonara

YIELDS 4 GENEROUS SERVINGS

Traditionally carbonara sauce is made with guanciale, or cured pork jowl, and served over spaghetti. I've opted for bucatini since it's so fun to eat and bacon because it's easier to find. Also I love the smokiness bacon adds to the silky sauce.

If you want to go all out, top each serving with a sunny-side-up fried egg.

Kosher salt

1 tablespoon (15 ml) extra-virgin olive oil

3 slices bacon, diced

1 clove garlic, grated using a fine rasp-style grater

Freshly ground black pepper

1 recipe fresh Semolina Bucatini (pages 78 and 85) or other sheeted or extruded pasta

4 to 5 eggs

2 oz (60 g) freshly grated, preferably using a rasp-style grater, Parmigiano-Reggiano, plus more for serving

3 green onions, sliced

Bring a large pot of water to a boil and salt generously.

Heat a large, heavy skillet over medium heat until hot. Add the olive oil and swirl to coat the inside of the pan. Add the bacon and fry, stirring frequently, until golden brown, crisp, and rendered, about 7 minutes. Remove from the heat and stir in the garlic and a generous grinding of pepper.

Add the pasta to the boiling water and boil, stirring frequently, until very nearly al dente. Blend together the eggs and Parmigiano in a medium bowl.

To finish the dish, reserve a ladleful of the pasta cooking water. Working quickly, drain the pasta, transfer it to the skillet with the bacon, add the egg mixture, and toss gently to coat, thinning with reserved pasta water as desired. The residual heat of the pasta will thicken up the eggs. Toss in the green onions. Serve immediately topped with additional Parmigiano.

Tartufo with Mushrooms Cacio e Pepe

YIELDS 4 GENEROUS SERVINGS

As if Cacio e Pepe could be improved upon . . . but I think I might've actually done it! This one recipe is worth the price of this book (even if you only make it with store-bought pasta). It may very well be my favorite recipe in this entire book, and that's saying a lot because I love them all!

If you are in the mood for a regular Cacio e Pepe, simply decrease the amount of olive oil to 1 tablespoon (15 ml) and skip the mushrooms and truffle oil.

Kosher salt

3 tablespoons (45 ml) extra-virgin olive oil

3 tablespoons (42 g) unsalted butter, diced

8 oz (225 g) button or cremini mushrooms, sliced

1 recipe fresh Semolina Spaghetti (pages 78 and 85) or other sheeted or extruded pasta

1 tablespoon (15 ml) freshly ground black pepper

1½–2 teaspoons (8–10 ml) truffle oil

3½ oz (100 g) freshly grated, preferably using a rasp-style grater, Pecorino Romano, plus more for serving

Bring a large pot of water to a boil and salt generously.

Heat a large, heavy skillet over medium heat until hot. Add the olive oil and butter and swirl to coat the inside of the pan. When the butter bubbles and the foam subsides, add the mushrooms. Sauté until tender and golden brown, about 7 minutes.

While the mushrooms finish sautéing, add the pasta to the boiling water and boil, stirring frequently, until nearly al dente.

To finish the dish, season the mushrooms lightly with salt. Nudge them to the side of the skillet and stir the pepper into the fat to toast. Reserve several ladlesful of the pasta cooking water. Working quickly, drain the pasta, transfer it to the skillet with sauce, add 1 cup (240 ml) of the reserved pasta water, and toss gently to coat. Remove from the heat and add the truffle oil and Pecorino. Toss gently, scraping the bottom of the pan using a heatproof spatula, until the Pecorino is melted into the sauce, thinning with additional pasta water as desired. Serve immediately topped with additional Pecorino.

Spaghetti with Anchovies

YIELDS 4 GENEROUS SERVINGS

Here's another dish that's usually made with boxed pasta, but the simplicity of the sauce makes it perfect for appreciating the flavor of homemade fresh pasta. The anchovies don't make it fishy, they just give it a deep umami quality.

Kosher salt

1 recipe fresh Semolina Spaghetti (pages 78 and 85) or other sheeted or extruded pasta

⅓ cup (80 ml) extra-virgin olive oil

4 large cloves garlic, minced

6–8 anchovy fillets, minced

Several generous pinches red chile flakes

¼ cup (15 g) minced Italian parsley

Freshly ground black pepper

Freshly squeezed juice of 1 small lemon

Crunchy Breadcrumbs (page 194), for serving

Freshly grated Parmigiano-Reggiano, for serving

Bring a large pot of water to a boil and salt generously.

Add the pasta to the boiling water and boil, stirring frequently, until nearly al dente.

While the pasta cooks, heat a large, heavy skillet over medium heat until hot. Add the olive oil and swirl to coat the inside of the pan. Add the garlic, anchovies, chile flakes, parlsey, and a generous grinding of pepper and sauté until the anchovies melt, about 1 minute.

To finish the dish, season the sauce with salt. Reserve a ladleful of the pasta cooking water. Working quickly, drain the pasta, transfer it to the skillet with sauce, add the lemon juice and ¼ cup (60 ml) of the reserved pasta water. Toss gently to coat, thinning with additional pasta water as desired. Remove from the heat and serve immediately topped with the Crunchy Breadcrumbs and plenty of grated Parmigiano.

Spaghetti with Quick Cherry Tomato Sauce and Fresh Mozzarella

YIELDS 4 GENEROUS SERVINGS

This dish is a favorite of mine and on the regular rotation at my house in the summer, when tomatoes are at their peak. I must confess that sometimes on busy weeknights I even make it with store-bought boxed pasta. It requires minimal time and effort and yet it's satisfying and delicious. It's particularly appetizing made with a colorful medley of cherry tomatoes.

Kosher salt

3 tablespoons (45 ml) extra-virgin olive oil, plus more for serving

4 cloves garlic, minced

Generous pinch red chile flakes

1 lb. 12 oz (800 g) yellow, orange, and red cherry tomatoes

1 recipe fresh Semolina Spaghetti (pages 78 and 85) or other sheeted or extruded pasta

1 large handful (about ¾ oz [20 g]) basil leaves, torn if large

Freshly ground black pepper

8 oz (225 g) fresh mozzarella pearls or diced bocconcini, drained and at room temperature

Freshly grated Parmigiano-Reggiano, for serving

Bring a large pot of water to a boil and salt generously.

Heat a large, heavy skillet over medium-low heat until hot. Add the olive oil and swirl to coat the inside of the pan. Add the garlic and chile flakes and sauté until fragrant, about 30 seconds. Add the tomatoes and cook, and stirring frequently, until they burst and their juices thicken, about 14 minutes. Help the tomatoes along by piercing them and smashing them lightly using a fork. This will also keep the splatter down from exploding tomatoes.

While the sauce finishes thickening, add the pasta to the boiling water and boil, stirring frequently, until nearly al dente.

To finish the dish, stir the basil into the sauce. Season with salt and pepper. Reserve a ladleful of the pasta cooking water. Working quickly, drain the pasta, transfer it to the skillet with sauce, and toss gently to coat, thinning with reserved pasta water as desired. Remove from the heat and serve immediately topped with the mozzarella, a generous drizzle of olive oil, and plenty of grated Parmigiano.

Spaghetti with Seafood Marinara

YIELDS 4 GENEROUS SERVINGS

This pasta is a veritable seafood feast. It's absolutely loaded with all the goodies—mussels, clams, shrimp, scallops, squid, and crabmeat, but believe it or not, the best part is the red sauce itself. Infusing the oil with the shrimp shells, which is a real chef move, gives the sauce an intensity of flavor that'll make seafood lovers swoon.

If at all possible, purchase seafood the day you intend to cook it. Mussels and clams are the most perishable, so before cooking, check that they're alive by giving any open ones a good tap. Discard any that do not close after a few moments. Then scrub with a stiff-bristled brush and pull off the coarse, fibrous beard from mussels. Also discard any mussels or clams that do not open once cooked.

Kosher salt

10⅔ oz (300 g) mussels

3 tablespoons (45 ml) extra-virgin olive oil

3 tablespoons (42 g) unsalted butter, diced

8 oz (225 g) 16–20 count shrimp, peeled, deveined, and shells reserved

1 bay leaf

1 allspice berry

3 cloves garlic, minced

Generous pinch red chile flakes

¼ cup (60 ml) white wine

½ recipe Slow-Simmered Tomato Sauce (page 109)

8 oz (225 g) Manila clams

1 recipe fresh Semolina Spaghetti (pages 78 and 85), Semolina and Oil Chitarra (pages 35 and 59), or other sheeted or extruded pasta

4 oz (110 g) bay scallops

4 oz (110 g) squid tubes and tentacles, tubes sliced into rings

Freshly ground black pepper

4 oz (110 g) Dungeness crabmeat, picked over

3 tablespoons (12 g) minced Italian parsley

Lemon wedges, for serving

Freshly grated Parmigiano-Reggiano, for serving, optional

Bring a large pot of water to a boil and salt generously.

Debeard the mussels.

Combine the olive oil, butter, shrimp shells, bay leaf, and allspice in a large, heavy pot. Heat over medium heat, stirring constantly, until the shrimp shells are pink and have a toasted aroma, about 5 minutes. Working quickly, remove the shrimp shells, bay leaf, and allspice using a slotted spoon and discard. Add the garlic and chile flakes to the pot and sauté until fragrant, about 30 seconds. Add the wine and simmer, stirring occasionally, until nearly dry, about 1 minute. Add the tomato sauce and bring to a boil, stirring occasionally. Add the mussels, clams, and shrimp. Return to a boil and simmer covered, stirring occasionally, until the mussels and clams open and the shrimp is pink, about 3 minutes.

While the mussels, clams, and shrimp simmer, add the pasta to the boiling water and boil, stirring frequently, until nearly al dente.

While the pasta finishes cooking, add the scallops and squid to the sauce. Return to a boil and simmer covered, stirring occasionally, until the scallops and squid are opaque, about 1 minute.

To finish the dish, season the sauce with salt and pepper. Reserve a ladleful of the pasta cooking water. Working quickly, drain the pasta, transfer it to the pot with the sauce, add the crab and parsley, and toss gently to coat, thinning with reserved pasta water as desired. Be conservative with the pasta water here—juice spilling from the mussels and clams will also thin the sauce at this point. Remove from the heat and discard any unopened mussels or clams. Serve immediately with the lemon wedges and topped with plenty of grated Parmigiano, if desired.

Spaghetti with Puttanesca Sauce

YIELDS 4 GENEROUS SERVINGS

Puttanesca is a classic pantry sauce that should be in every cook's repertoire. The dish requires little effort or time, and yet the combination of umami-rich ingredients packs a ton of flavor.

Kosher salt

2 tablespoons (30 ml) extra-virgin olive oil

4 cloves garlic, minced

3 anchovy fillets, minced

Generous pinch red chile flakes

1 can (28 oz [794 g]) whole peeled tomatoes, preferably San Marzanos

½ cup (64 g) pitted Kalamata olives, sliced

3 tablespoons (27 g) capers

1 recipe fresh Semolina Spaghetti (pages 78 and 85) or other sheeted or extruded pasta

Freshly ground black pepper

¼ cup (15 g) minced Italian parsley

Freshly grated Parmigiano-Reggiano, for serving

Bring a large pot of water to a boil and salt generously.

Heat a large, heavy skillet over medium heat until hot. Add the olive oil and swirl to coat the inside of the pan. Add the garlic, anchovies, and chile flakes. Sauté until fragrant, about 30 seconds. Add the tomatoes along with their liquid, olives, and capers. Simmer, stirring occasionally and breaking up the tomatoes with the back of a spoon, until thickened, about 18 minutes.

While the sauce finishes thickening, add the pasta to the boiling water and boil, stirring frequently, until nearly al dente.

To finish the dish, season the sauce with salt and pepper. Reserve a ladleful of the pasta cooking water. Working quickly, drain the pasta and transfer it to the skillet with the sauce. Add the parsley and toss gently to coat, thinning with reserved pasta water as desired. Remove from the heat and serve immediately topped with plenty of grated Parmigiano.

Tuna Variation: Use 1 can (8¾ ounces, or 250 g) of best quality canned oil-packed tuna, such as Spanish Bonito del Norte. Drain the tuna, reserving the oil, and flake it. Substitute the oil from the tuna for the olive oil and add the tuna to the sauce at the same time as the pasta and parsley.

Linguine with Tomato and Ricotta Sauce

YIELDS 4 GENEROUS SERVINGS

This is a flash-in-the-pan recipe that's wonderful in the summer, when sweet and juicy ripe tomatoes are plentiful. A generous spoonful of ricotta stirred into the pasta just as it's done makes it rich, creamy, and delicious.

Kosher salt

3 tablespoons (45 ml) extra-virgin olive oil

½ red onion, julienned

1 jalapeño, sliced

4 cloves garlic, minced

13 oz (370 g) cocktail tomatoes, diced

½ teaspoon dried oregano

1 recipe fresh Semolina Linguine (pages 78 and 85) or other sheeted, extruded, or cavatelli maker pasta

1 tablespoon (15 ml) vodka

Freshly ground black pepper

5⅓ oz (150 g) Homemade Ricotta (page 191) or store-bought, at room temperature

Freshly grated Parmigiano-Reggiano, for serving

Bring a large pot of water to a boil and salt generously.

Heat a large, heavy skillet over medium heat until hot. Add the olive oil and swirl to coat the inside of the pan. Add the onion and sauté until beginning to brown, about 4 minutes. Add the jalapeño and sauté until beginning to soften, about 1 minute. Add the garlic and sauté until fragrant, about 30 seconds. Add the tomatoes and oregano. Cook until the tomato juices thicken, about 4 minutes.

While the sauce thickens, add the pasta to the boiling water and boil, stirring frequently, until very nearly al dente.

To finish the dish, stir the vodka into the sauce, remove it from the heat, and season it with salt and pepper. Reserve a ladleful of the pasta cooking water. Working quickly, drain the pasta and transfer it to the skillet with sauce. Add the ricotta and toss gently to coat, thinning with reserved pasta water as desired. Serve immediately topped with plenty of grated Parmigiano.

Rigatoni with Smoky Arrabbiata Sauce

YIELDS 4 GENEROUS SERVINGS

Arrabbiata means "angry" in Italian, and here it refers to the liberal use of red chile flakes. Use more or less chile according to your taste to adjust the heat level from slightly angry to quite furious. Bacon lends a hint of smokiness.

Kosher salt

1 tablespoon (15 ml) extra-virgin olive oil

4 slices bacon, diced

1 small yellow onion, diced

4 cloves garlic, minced

Generous pinch red chile flakes

1 can (28 oz [794 g]) whole peeled tomatoes, preferably San Marzanos

1 recipe fresh Semolina Rigatoni (pages 78 and 85) or other sheeted, extruded, or cavatelli maker pasta

Freshly ground black pepper

Freshly grated Pecorino Romano, Parmigiano-Reggiano, or a blend of the two, for serving

Bring a large pot of water to a boil and salt generously.

Heat a large, heavy skillet over medium-low heat until hot. Add the olive oil and swirl to coat the inside of the pan. Add the bacon and fry, stirring frequently, until golden brown, crisp, and rendered, about 7 minutes. Add the onion and sauté until soft, about 5 minutes. Add the garlic and chile flakes and sauté until fragrant, about 30 seconds. Add the tomatoes along with their liquid and simmer, stirring occasionally and breaking up the tomatoes with the back of a spoon, until thickened, about 18 minutes.

While the sauce finishes thickening, add the pasta to the boiling water and boil, stirring frequently, until nearly al dente.

To finish the dish, season the sauce with salt and pepper. Reserve a ladleful of the pasta cooking water. Working quickly, drain the pasta, transfer it to the skillet with the sauce, and toss gently to coat, thinning with reserved pasta water as desired. Remove from the heat and serve immediately topped with plenty of grated cheese.

Rigatoni with Chickpeas

YIELDS 4 GENEROUS SERVINGS

Pasta and beans with and rosemary-scented tomato sauce is a hearty and satisfying combination. This is a vegetarian dish, and nobody ever seems to miss the meat.

The flavor of chickpeas, and in fact of pretty much all beans, is better when they are not soaked before cooking. Just keep in mind that cooking time for unsoaked dried chickpeas can vary from just a couple of hours to more than 3 hours, depending on how fresh they are, so check for doneness early and often. You can substitute canned chickpeas in a pinch.

1 cup (250 g) chickpeas, picked over

1 clove garlic, crushed lightly, plus 3 cloves, minced

1 bay leaf

¼ cup (60 ml) plus 1 tablespoon (15 ml) extra-virgin olive oil, divided, plus more for serving

Freshly ground black pepper

Kosher salt

½ yellow onion, diced

Generous pinch red chile flakes

1 can (28 oz [794 g]) whole peeled tomatoes, preferably San Marzanos

2 sprigs rosemary

1 recipe fresh Semolina Rigatoni (pages 78 and 85) or other sheeted, extruded, or cavatelli maker pasta

Freshly grated Pecorino Romano, Parmigiano-Reggiano, or a blend of the two, for serving

Combine the chickpeas, crushed garlic, bay leaf, 1 tablespoon (15 ml) of the olive oil, a generous grinding of black pepper, and enough water to cover by several inches in a small, heavy saucepan. Bring to a boil, season with salt, and simmer, adding water as necessary to keep the chickpeas submerged, until the chickpeas are tender, about 3 hours.

While the chickpeas finish simmering, bring a large pot of water to a boil and salt generously.

Drain the chickpeas, reserving the cooking liquid for another use, and discard the bay leaf. Mash about one-third of the chickpeas.

Heat a large, heavy skillet over medium-low heat until hot. Add the remaining olive oil and swirl to coat the inside of the pan. Add the onion and sauté until soft, about 5 minutes. Add the minced garlic and chile flakes and sauté until fragrant, about 30 seconds. Add the tomatoes along with their liquid, whole and mashed chickpeas, and rosemary. Simmer, stirring occasionally and breaking up the tomatoes with the back of a spoon, until thickened, about 16 minutes.

While the sauce finishes thickening, add the pasta to the boiling water and boil, stirring frequently, until nearly al dente.

To finish the dish, season the sauce with salt and pepper and discard the rosemary sprigs. Reserve a ladleful of the pasta cooking water. Working quickly, drain the pasta, transfer it to the skillet with the sauce, and toss gently to coat, thinning with reserved pasta water as desired. Remove from the heat and serve immediately topped with plenty of grated cheese and a generous drizzle of olive oil.

Penne with Roasted Red Pepper-Tomato Sauce and Burrata

YIELDS 4 GENEROUS SERVINGS

When I was a teenager, my parents took me out to lunch at a fancy Italian restaurant. I ordered the penne in creamy tomato sauce, which came studded with cubes of fresh mozzarella. It must've been my first exposure to proper al dente pasta and also my first taste of fresh mozzarella. The memory it is so vivid I can almost taste it—toothsome pasta and sweet, milky, tender, and barely-warm-enough-to-melt fresh mozzarella smothered in a sweet and acidic tomato sauce redolent of basil. It was love at first bite. If a meal could be a formative experience, then this was mine. Looking back on it, it was one of the things that set me down the pasta path.

The restaurant has long since closed, but decades later I've cooked many a meal inspired by it. This is my favorite riff, with roasted bell pepper for an added dimension. And I've upgraded the fresh mozzarella to burrata. Another tasty variation is thinning the sauce with water and serving it as a soup with pastina instead of penne.

1 large red bell pepper

¾ cup (175 ml) heavy cream

Kosher salt

2 tablespoons (30 ml) extra-virgin olive oil, plus more for serving

3 cloves garlic, minced

Generous pinch red chile flakes

1 carton (26 oz [750 g]) strained tomatoes, such as Pomi

1 large handful (about ¾ oz [20 g]) basil leaves, torn if large

1 recipe fresh Semolina Penne (pages 78 and 85) or other sheeted, extruded, or cavatelli maker pasta

Freshly ground black pepper

2 balls (4 oz [115 g] each) burrata

Freshly grated Parmigiano-Reggiano, for serving

Coarse sea salt, such as Maldon or fleur de sel, for serving

Place the pepper directly on a grate over a gas burner set to high heat and cook, turning occasionally, until charred and blistered all over, about 9 minutes. Transfer to a bowl, cover tightly with plastic wrap to trap the steam, and let cool. Transfer to a cutting board, scrape off the skin using a paring knife, seed, and chop coarsely. Transfer the pepper along with any accumulated juice to a blender, add the cream, and blend just until smooth.

Bring a large pot of water to a boil and salt generously.

Heat a large, heavy skillet over medium-low heat until hot. Add the olive oil and swirl to coat the inside of the pan. Add the garlic and chile flakes and sauté until fragrant, about 30 seconds. Add the tomatoes, pepper purée, and basil. Bring to a boil and simmer, stirring frequently, until thickened, about 25 minutes.

While the sauce finishes thickening, add the pasta to the boiling water and boil, stirring frequently, until nearly al dente.

To finish the dish, season the sauce with salt and pepper. Gently cut each ball of burrata in half. Reserve a ladleful of the pasta cooking water. Working quickly, drain the pasta, transfer it to the skillet with sauce, and toss gently to coat, thinning with reserved pasta water as desired. Remove from the heat and serve immediately topped with plenty of grated Parmigiano, the burrata, a generous drizzle of olive oil, and a sprinkling of sea salt.

Macaroni alla Norma

YIELDS 4 GENEROUS SERVINGS

This classic pasta in a red sauce with eggplant comes from Sicily. Traditionally the eggplant is fried but I prefer to roast it in the oven as it is much less fussy and every bit as delicious.

Though it is a vegetarian dish, the meaty eggplant tends to satisfy carnivores.

½ cup (120 ml) extra-virgin olive oil, divided

1 large Globe eggplant, cut into 1-inch (2.5-cm) pieces

Kosher salt

Freshly ground black pepper

3 cloves garlic, minced

Generous pinch red chile flakes

1 can (28 oz [794 g]) whole peeled tomatoes, preferably San Marzanos

1 large handful (about ¾ oz [20 g]) basil leaves, torn if large

1 tablespoon (4 g) minced oregano

1 recipe fresh Semolina Macaroni (pages 78 and 85) or other sheeted, extruded, or cavatelli maker pasta

Freshly grated ricotta salata, for serving

Preheat the oven to 425°F (220°C, or gas mark 6).

Drizzle 6 tablespoons (90 ml) of the olive oil all over a baking sheet. Add the eggplant and turn to coat. The eggplant will soak up the oil like a sponge, but work quickly and try to get it coated as evenly as possible. Season with salt and pepper. Roast until meltingly tender and golden brown, about 30 minutes.

While the eggplant roasts, bring a large pot of water to a boil and salt generously.

Heat a large, heavy skillet over medium heat until hot. Add the remaining 2 tablespoons (30 ml) of olive oil and swirl to coat the inside of the pan. Add the garlic and chile flakes and sauté until fragrant, about 30 seconds. Add the tomatoes along with their liquid, basil, and oregano. Simmer, stirring occasionally and breaking up the tomatoes with the back of a spoon, until thickened, about 18 minutes.

While the sauce finishes thickening, add the pasta to the boiling water and boil, stirring frequently, until nearly al dente.

To finish the dish, add the eggplant to the sauce and season with salt and pepper. Reserve a ladleful of the pasta cooking water. Working quickly, drain the pasta, transfer it to the skillet with the sauce, and toss gently to coat, thinning with reserved pasta water as desired. Remove from the heat and serve immediately topped with plenty of grated ricotta salata.

Fusilli with Salsa Cruda

YIELDS 4 GENEROUS SERVINGS

Salsa cruda is simply an uncooked tomato sauce. It is the thing to make in the summer with peak of the season sweet and juicy heirloom tomatoes. It's often made with skin-on tomatoes, but skinning and draining the tomatoes gives the sauce a much nicer texture.

Kosher salt

2 lb. (905 g) heirloom tomatoes

¼ cup (60 ml) extra-virgin olive oil

2 cloves garlic, grated using a rasp-style grater

1 recipe fresh Semolina Fusilli (pages 78 and 85) or other sheeted, extruded, or cavatelli maker pasta

Freshly ground black pepper

1 small handful (about ⅓ oz [10 g]) basil leaves, torn if large

Freshly grated Parmigiano-Reggiano, for serving

Bring a large pot of water to a boil and salt generously.

Cut a 1-inch (2.5-cm) X through the skin of the blossom end of each tomato using a paring knife. Add a couple of the tomatoes to the boiling water and boil until the skins loosen, about 20 seconds. Using a wire skimmer, remove the tomatoes from the pot and transfer to a large bowl of ice water to cool as quickly as possible. Boil the remaining tomatoes in the same manner. Remove the tomatoes from the ice water, blot dry with paper towels, and slip off the skins. Dice the tomatoes and drain them in a fine-mesh sieve, reserving the juice for another use (such as substituting it for water in a batch of pasta!).

Blend together the olive oil and garlic. Stir in the tomatoes.

Return the water to a boil. Add the pasta and boil, stirring frequently, until very nearly al dente.

To finish the dish, season the sauce with salt and pepper. Working quickly, drain the pasta and return it to the pot (off the heat). Add the sauce and basil and toss gently to coat. Serve immediately topped with plenty of grated Parmigiano.

Caprese Variation: Serve the pasta topped with 8 ounces (225 g) of drained, room-temperature fresh mozzarella pearls or diced bocconcini and a generous drizzle of real balsamic vinegar.

BLT Variation: Add several strips of crumbled bacon and 5 ounces (140 g) of baby spinach or arugula to the pasta at the same time as the sauce.

Fusilli with Olive-Caper Sauce

If you like tapenade, then you will certainly want to try this pasta. The uncooked sauce is light and perfect on a hot summer day.

Kosher salt

¾ cup (96 g) pitted Kalamata olives

¼ cup (36 g) capers

1 clove garlic, sliced

⅓ cup (80 ml) extra-virgin olive oil

Freshly ground black pepper

1 recipe fresh Semolina Fusilli (pages 78 and 85) or other sheeted, extruded, or cavatelli maker pasta

14 oz (400 g) cherry tomatoes, quartered

1 large handful (about ¾ oz [20 g]) basil leaves, torn if large

Freshly grated Parmigiano-Reggiano, for serving

Bring a large pot of water to a boil and salt generously.

Combine the olives, capers, and garlic in a food processor and process until smooth. Add the olive oil and pulse to combine. Season with pepper.

Add the pasta to the boiling water and boil, stirring frequently, until very nearly al dente.

To finish the dish, reserve a ladleful of the pasta cooking water. Working quickly, drain the pasta and return it to the pot (off the heat). Add the sauce, tomatoes, and basil. Toss gently to coat, thinning with reserved pasta water as desired. Serve immediately topped with plenty of grated Parmigiano.

Antipasto Pasta

YIELDS 4 TO 6 SERVINGS

The name of this dish might make an Italian snicker—antipasto means starter or *before the meal*, after all—but it's like an entire antipasto platter turned pasta salad. It's a great make-ahead recipe, perfect for picnics and potlucks.

Kosher salt

2 tablespoons (30 ml) red wine vinegar

2 teaspoons (10 g) Dijon mustard

1 large clove garlic, grated using a rasp-style grater

½ teaspoon dried basil

½ teaspoon dried oregano

⅓ cup (80 ml) extra-virgin olive oil

Freshly ground black pepper

1 recipe fresh Semolina Fusilli (pages 78 and 85) or other short-cut extruded pasta

8¾ oz (250 g) cherry tomatoes, halved

8 oz (225 g) fresh mozzarella pearls or diced bocconcini, drained

7 oz (200 g) pepperoni or other salami, diced

1 can (13¾ oz [390 g]) artichoke hearts, drained

½ cup (120 g) Homemade Oil-Packed Pickled Peppers along with their oil (page 192)

½ cup (64 g) Kalamata olives, halved

½ small red onion, diced

1 small handful (about ⅓ oz [10 g]) basil leaves, torn if large

1¾ oz (50 g) freshly grated Parmigiano-Reggiano

Bring a large pot of water to a boil and salt generously.

Whisk together the vinegar, mustard, garlic, basil, and oregano in a medium bowl. Whisk in the olive oil in a thin stream, and season with salt and pepper.

Add the pasta to the boiling water and boil, stirring frequently, until nearly al dente.

Working quickly, drain the pasta. With the pasta still in the colander, run cold water over it while gently separating the pieces to cool as quickly as possible and rinse away excess starch. Drain the pasta thoroughly. Immediately combine the pasta, tomatoes, mozzarella, pepperoni, artichoke hearts, pickled peppers, olives, onion, basil leaves, and the dressing in a large bowl. Toss gently to coat. Cover and marinate 1 to 2 hours, tossing occasionally.

To finish the dish, toss in the Parmigiano and serve.

Pasta with Italian Sausage, Butternut Squash, and Sage

YIELDS 4 GENEROUS SERVINGS

This is one of my favorite pasta dishes for the fall. It's one of the first things I make every year when the butternut squash appears at the market. It's so simple and yet sophisticated enough for a formal dinner party—when I was still working in the industry as a chef, I even served it as part of a fancy wine dinner and it stole the show!

Personally I like to simmer everything together until the cubes of butternut squash lose their hard edges and start to melt into the sauce. I might even mash a couple of the pieces of squash because the purée makes the sauce all the more luscious.

Kosher salt

3 tablespoons (45 ml) extra-virgin olive oil

1 lb. (455 g) Homemade Bulk Spicy Italian Sausage (page 188) or store-bought, broken up

3 cloves garlic, minced

Generous pinch red chile flakes

2 tablespoons (5 g) minced sage

1 medium (about 2 lb. 4 oz [1030 g]) butternut squash, cut into 1-inch (2.5-cm) pieces

1 cup (240 ml) Simple Chicken Stock (page 195)

Freshly ground black pepper

1 recipe fresh Semolina Penne (pages 78 and 85), Butternut Squash Cavatelli (page 94 and 97), or other short-cut sheeted or extruded or cavatelli maker pasta

Freshly grated Parmigiano-Reggiano, for serving

Bring a large pot of water to a boil and salt generously.

Heat a large, heavy skillet over medium-high heat until hot. Add the olive oil and swirl to coat the inside of the pan. Add the sausage and fry, stirring occasionally, until golden brown, about 6 minutes. Add the garlic, chile flakes, and sage, and sauté until fragrant, about 30 seconds. Add the butternut squash and stock and simmer covered, stirring occasionally, until the squash is extremely soft, about 20 minutes.

While the squash finishes cooking, add the pasta to the boiling water and boil, stirring frequently, until nearly al dente.

To finish the dish, season the sauce with salt and pepper. Reserve a ladleful of the pasta cooking water. Working quickly, drain the pasta, transfer it to the skillet with the sauce, and toss gently to coat, thinning with reserved pasta water as desired. Remove from the heat and serve immediately topped with plenty of grated Parmigiano.

Cavatelli with Broccoli Sauce

YIELDS 4 GENEROUS SERVINGS

Cavatelli is the perfect vehicle for a thick sauce of broccoli purée that's flavored with anchovy and lots of garlic. Even though it's green my meat-eating husband loves it!

Kosher salt

¼ cup (60 ml) extra-virgin olive oil

4 cloves garlic, minced

2 anchovy fillets

Generous pinch red chile flakes

1 lb. 8 oz (670 g) broccoli, florets separated; stems peeled and chopped coarsely

Freshly ground black pepper

1 recipe fresh Cavatelli (page 92 and 97) or other sheeted, extruded, or cavatelli maker pasta

Crunchy Breadcrumbs (page 194), for serving, optional

Freshly grated Pecorino Romano, Parmigiano-Reggiano, or a blend of the two, for serving

Bring a large pot of water to a boil and salt generously.

Heat a large, heavy skillet over medium-low heat until hot. Add the olive oil and swirl to coat the inside of the pan. Add the garlic, anchovies, and chile flakes, and sauté until fragrant, about 30 seconds. Add the broccoli and ½ cup (120 ml) of water. Bring to a boil and simmer covered, stirring occasionally, until the broccoli is very tender, about 14 minutes. Transfer to a food processor and process until smooth. Season with salt and pepper.

Add the pasta to the boiling water and boil, stirring frequently, until very nearly al dente.

To finish the dish, reserve a ladleful of the pasta cooking water. Working quickly, drain the pasta and return it to the pot (off the heat). Add the sauce and toss gently to coat, thinning with reserved pasta water as desired. Serve immediately topped with the Crunchy Breadcrumbs, if desired, and plenty of grated cheese.

Feta Variation: Add 5 ounces (140 g) sharp feta to the food processor at the same time as the broccoli.

Cavatelli with Spicy Italian Sausage, Broccoli Raab, and Pickled Peppers

YIELDS 4 GENEROUS SERVINGS

This recipe, based on a classic flavor combination, is marvelously easy because the pasta and the vegetables are all boiled together right in the same pot. And yet the result is delicious: a chunky and satisfying pasta that's loaded with bold flavor.

Substitute broccoli or kale if you can't get your hands on raab.

Kosher salt

⅓ cup (80 ml) extra-virgin olive oil

1 lb. (455 g) Homemade Bulk Spicy Italian Sausage (page 188) or store-bought, broken up

1 recipe fresh Cavatelli (page 92 and 97) or other sheeted, extruded, or cavatelli maker pasta

1 large bunch broccoli raab, cut into bite-size pieces

4 cloves garlic, minced

Generous pinch red chile flakes

Freshly ground black pepper

½ cup (120 g) Homemade Oil-Packed Pickled Peppers along with their oil (page 192)

Freshly grated Pecorino Romano, for serving

Bring a large pot of water to a boil and salt generously.

Heat a large, heavy skillet over medium-high heat until hot. Add the olive oil and swirl to coat the inside of the pan. Add the sausage and fry, stirring occasionally, until golden brown, about 6 minutes.

While the sausage browns, add the pasta and raab to the boiling water. Boil, stirring frequently, until the pasta is nearly al dente and the raab is tender.

To finish the dish, add the garlic and chile flakes to the skillet with the sausage. Sauté until fragrant, about 30 seconds. Season with salt and pepper. Reserve a ladleful of the pasta cooking water. Working quickly, drain the pasta and raab, then transfer them to the skillet with the sauce. Add the pickled peppers and toss gently to coat, thinning with reserved pasta water as desired. Remove from the heat and serve immediately topped with plenty of grated Pecorino.

Lamburger Helper

YIELDS 4 GENEROUS SERVINGS

Here's a pasta dish with flavors of the Middle East. It is fragrant with warm spices and cilantro. Despite the somewhat exotic inspiration, it is quick, easy, and hearty, as the name suggests.

Along with jalapeño, Aleppo pepper, which comes from Syria, infuses this dish with a mild spiciness. It is available at Mediterranean and Middle Eastern markets, spice shops, and at most gourmet grocers.

Kosher salt

3 tablespoons (45 ml) extra-virgin olive oil

1 lb. (455 g) ground lamb, broken up

½ red onion, diced

1 jalapeño, minced

3 cloves garlic, minced

2 teaspoons (4 g) Aleppo pepper

2 teaspoons (5 g) ground coriander

1½ teaspoons (4 g) ground cumin

1 can (14½ oz [411 g]) diced tomatoes

1 recipe fresh Cavatelli (page 92 and 97) or other extruded or cavatelli maker pasta

Freshly ground black pepper

⅓ cup (5 g) minced cilantro

Crumbled sharp feta, for serving

Bring a large pot of water to a boil and salt generously.

Heat a large, heavy skillet over medium-high heat until hot. Add the olive oil and swirl to coat the inside of the pot. Add the lamb and sear, tossing a couple of times, until golden brown all over, about 8 minutes. Remove the lamb to a plate using a slotted spoon. Lower the heat to medium-low and add the onion to the skillet. Sauté until soft, about 5 minutes. Add the jalapeño and sauté until soft, about 2 minutes. Add the garlic, Aleppo pepper, coriander, and cumin, and sauté until fragrant, about 30 seconds. Add the tomatoes along with their liquid and return the lamb along with any accumulated juice to the skillet. Simmer, stirring occasionally, until thickened, about 5 minutes.

While the sauce finishes thickening, add the pasta to the boiling water and boil, stirring frequently, until nearly al dente.

To finish the dish, season the sauce with salt and pepper. Reserve a ladleful of the pasta cooking water. Working quickly, drain the pasta, transfer it to the pot with the sauce, add the cilantro, and toss gently to coat, thinning with reserved pasta water as desired. Remove from the heat and serve immediately topped with plenty of crumbled feta.

Malloreddus with Pork and Pepper Ragu

YIELDS 4 GENEROUS SERVINGS

With saffron and fennel pollen, this dish is a little different from your typical pork ragu.

Fennel pollen, which tastes milder and sweeter than fennel seed, is available at most gourmet grocers and online.

3 tablespoons (45 ml) extra-virgin olive oil

1 lb. (455 g) ground pork, broken up

1 yellow onion, diced

1 green bell pepper, diced

4 cloves garlic, minced

Generous pinch red chile flakes

1 can (28 oz [794 g]) whole peeled tomatoes, preferably San Marzanos

2 teaspoons (2 g) fennel pollen

Generous pinch saffron

⅓ cup (80 g) Homemade Oil-Packed Pickled Peppers along with their oil

Kosher salt

1 recipe fresh Malloreddus (page 95 and 97) or other sheeted, extruded, or cavatelli maker pasta

Freshly ground black pepper

Freshly grated Pecorino Romano, for serving

Heat a large, heavy pot over medium-high heat until hot. Add the olive oil and swirl to coat the inside of the pot. Add the pork and sear, tossing a couple of times, until golden brown all over, about 8 minutes. Remove the pork to a plate using a slotted spoon. Lower the heat to medium-low and add the onion to the pot. Sauté until beginning to soften, about 6 minutes. Add the bell pepper and sauté until soft, about 5 minutes. Add the garlic and chile flakes. Sauté until fragrant, about 30 seconds. Add the tomatoes along with their liquid and the fennel pollen, saffron, and pickled peppers. Return the pork along with any accumulated juice to the pot. Simmer, stirring occasionally and breaking up the tomatoes with the back of a spoon, until thickened, about 40 minutes.

While the sauce simmers, bring a large pot of water to a boil and salt generously.

While the sauce finishes thickening, add the pasta to the boiling water and boil, stirring frequently, until nearly al dente.

To finish the dish, season the sauce with salt and pepper. Reserve a ladle-ful of the pasta cooking water. Working quickly, drain the pasta, transfer it to the pot with the sauce, and toss gently to coat, thinning with reserved pasta water as desired. Remove from the heat and serve immediately topped with plenty of grated Pecorino.

Italian Sausage Variation: Substitute Homemade Bulk Spicy Italian Sausage (page 188) or store-bought for the ground pork.

Grano Arso Cavatelli with Sundried Tomato Sauce

YIELDS 4 GENEROUS SERVINGS

This pasta has a quick uncooked sauce, and you likely have all of the ingredients in your pantry already. With savory sundried tomatoes, olives, optional anchovies, and Parmigiano, it is an umami bomb that's good enough to eat straight up by the spoonful. Consider making a double or triple batch of the sauce to stash some in the fridge for another night. You'll thank yourself later.

Kosher salt

3 oz (85 g) sundried tomatoes

¼ cup (32 g) pitted Kalamata olives

1-2 anchovy fillets, optional

1 large handful (about ¾ oz [20 g]) basil leaves

1¼ oz (35 g) freshly grated Parmigiano-Reggiano, plus more for serving

2 cloves garlic, sliced

Generous pinch red chile flakes

⅓ cup (80 ml) extra-virgin olive oil

Freshly ground black pepper

1 recipe fresh Grano Arso Cavatelli (page 95 and 97), Whole Durum Rigatoni (pages 81 and 85), or other sheeted, extruded, or cavatelli maker pasta

Bring a large pot of water to a boil and salt generously.

Combine the sundried tomatoes and just enough boiling water to cover in a medium bowl. Let soak until rehydrated and pliable, about 15 minutes. Transfer the sundried tomatoes along with their soaking water to a blender, add the olives, anchovies, if desired, basil, Parmigiano, garlic, chile flakes, and olive oil. Blend until smooth. Season with salt and pepper.

Add the pasta to the boiling water and boil, stirring frequently, until very nearly al dente.

To finish the dish, reserve a ladleful of the pasta cooking water. Working quickly, drain the pasta and return it to the pot (off the heat). Add the sauce and toss gently to coat, thinning with reserved pasta water as desired. Serve immediately topped with additional Parmigiano.

Cannoli

YIELDS APPROXIMATELY 24 CANNOLI

Cannoli dough is quite similar to pasta dough, except it has a high proportion of fat in the dough to make it short and tender and it is fried rather than boiled. This particular cannoli recipe includes lots of egg yolks and butter and also a splash of wine. The shells are light and ethereal, and the filling is fluffy and not too sweet.

When sheeting the cannoli dough, I recommend using the same thickness setting as you would for noodles.

The hardest part of making cannoli is getting the shells off the molds intact. I find that the best method is to stand the still-warm mold on its end. Hold the top of the mold with one hand and grasp the cannoli with your other hand—use your whole hand, palm and all, wrapping your fingers all the way around it, and then firmly but carefully slide it down the mold. Getting it to budge is the hardest part but then it'll slip right off.

Cannoli shells may be fried and the filling may be mixed several hours in advance. Fill the shells just before serving so that they do not become soggy.

(continued)

(Cannoli continued)

FOR THE DOUGH:

200 g (7 oz) unbleached
all-purpose flour

Generous pinch kosher salt

1 egg, at room temperature

3 yolks, at room temperature

30 g (1 oz) unsalted butter, melted

15 g (½ oz) white wine, at room
temperature

10 g (⅓ oz) water, at room
temperature

FOR FRYING:

½ quarts (1.4 L) canola oil

FOR THE FILLING:

1 lb. (455 g) Homemade Ricotta
(page 191) or store-bought,
at room temperature

2 oz (55 g) powdered sugar

½ teaspoon grated, using
a rasp-style grater, lemon zest

¼ teaspoon pure vanilla extract

Generous pinch cinnamon

4 oz (110 g) heavy cream, chilled

Chopped pistachios, for serving

Toasted sliced almonds, for serving

Grated dark chocolate, for serving

FOR THE DOUGH:

Mix, wrap, and rest the dough in the same manner as any other sheeted pasta (page 40). Cut the dough into quarters and sheet it relatively thick, just under ¹⁄₁₆ inches (1½ mm). Cut the sheeted dough into circles using a 3½-inch (8½-cm) cookie cutter. As you work, keep the dough covered to prevent it from drying out.

FOR FRYING:

Heat the canola oil in a large, heavy pot to 375°F (190°C).

While the oil heats, grease the cannoli molds with a few drops of the canola oil. Place a cannoli mold in the center of a dough circle and roll the dough around the mold, not too tight and not too loose. Using a fingertip, lightly moisten the overlapping dough with water—just the smallest amount of water will do—and press firmly to seal. Form 5 more cannoli shells in the same manner. Add the cannoli shells to the hot oil and deep-fry until golden brown, about 3 minutes. Using a pair of tweezer-tongs and a wire skimmer, remove the cannoli shells to a paper towel–lined sheet tray and let drain and cool. When the shells are just cool enough to handle, carefully but with the courage of your convictions remove them from the molds. Reheat the oil and form, fry, and unmold the remaining cannoli shells in 3 more batches of 6 in the same manner. Let the cannoli shells cool to room temperature.

FOR THE FILLING:

To finish the cannoli, blend together the ricotta, powdered sugar, lemon zest, vanilla, and cinnamon. Whip the cream to medium peaks and gently fold into the ricotta mixture. Transfer the filling to a pastry bag fitted with a large plain tip. Pipe the filling into the cannoli shells from both ends. Dip the ends of the cannoli into the pistachios, almonds, or chocolate to coat as desired. Serve immediately.

Semolina Crackers

YIELDS APPROXIMATELY 6 DOZEN CRACKERS

Homemade crackers are infinitely better than store-bought, and they are of course the perfect accompaniment to cheese. And the good news is that if you know how to make pasta from scratch, you also know how to make crackers from scratch. The only difference, really, is that crackers are baked instead of boiled.

When sheeting the cracker dough, I recommend using the same thickness setting as you would for noodles.

---

170 g (6 oz) semolina

170 g (6 oz) unbleached all-purpose flour

4 g (1½ teaspoons) kosher salt, plus more for sprinkling

170 g (6 oz) water, preferably lukewarm

20 g (¾ oz) extra-virgin olive oil, plus more for brushing

Mix, wrap, and rest the dough in the same manner as any other sheeted pasta (pages 40–44). Cut the dough into sixths and sheet it relatively thick, just under 1/16 inch (1½ mm).

Transfer the sheeted dough to parchment-lined baking sheets. Brush generously with olive oil, and cut into individual crackers using a pastry wheel as desired (no need to separate individual crackers). Sprinkle generously with salt. Bake until toasted, golden brown, and crisp, about 20 minutes depending on thickness. Let cool to room temperature and snap the individual crackers apart.

Well-toasted crackers will keep for a week or two tightly sealed in the pantry.

Seeded/Spiced Crackers: Blend 2 teaspoons to 1 tablespoon (3 to 8 g) sesame seeds, poppy seeds, nigella seeds, red chile flakes, or coarse freshly ground black pepper with the dry ingredients before mixing the dough.

Rosemary Crackers: Blend 2 tablespoons (4 g) of rosemary needles with the dry ingredients before mixing the dough.

Parmigiano Crackers: Sprinkle the dough generously with freshly grated Parmigiano-Reggiano after brushing with olive oil and sprinkling with salt and before baking.

CHAPTER 6

Pantry and Fridge Staples for Pasta Cooks

Homemade Bulk Spicy Italian Sausage

YIELDS ABOUT 908 G (2 POUNDS)

If the Tartufo with Mushrooms Cacio e Pepe (page 158) recipe alone is worth the price of this book, then the Homemade Spicy Italian Sausage was worth the price of my last book *Not Your Mother's Cast Iron Skillet Cookbook*, where the recipe first appeared. I'm including the recipe again here because if you're making fresh pasta, then you certainly need an outstanding sausage to go in your ragus and sauces. This recipe is significant upgrade over store-bought sausage, and it's also surprisingly easy to make.

Wild fennel seed, which is usually imported from Italy, has a lovely sweet quality and can be found online.

When making fresh sausage, do not use ground pork with a lower fat content or the result will be dry and flavorless.

Just as with pasta dough hydration percentages (page 12), grams and percentages are used for sausage recipes for the most ease, accuracy, and flexibility. As long as you have a scale that works in grams, it's very simple to do and you don't even need to know any conversions. All of the ingredients are expressed as a percentage of the weight of the ground meat. For example, if you'd like to make a small batch of sausage with just 300 grams (10⅔ ounces) of ground pork, you can calculate that you need 5.3 grams of kosher salt by multiplying 300 grams by 1.75%. Using percentages allows you to figure out exactly how much of each ingredient you need whatever the weight of ground pork you start with.

Keep all equipment and ingredients well chilled, and mix until thoroughly blended and visibly sticky to ensure proper emulsification. Stickiness is a sign that the proteins have bound with the liquid in the meat and the emulsion is set. The result when cooked is juicy sausage that holds together because fat won't render as readily.

You can cook the sausage as soon as it is mixed, but the flavor benefits from being refrigerated overnight.

PERCENTAGE	AMOUNT FOR 908 GRAMS (2 LBS.) GROUND PORK	
100%	908 g (2.00 lb.)	20 to 30% fat ground pork, broken up
1.75%	15.9 g (0.56 oz)	kosher salt
0.5%	4.5 g (0.16 oz)	fennel seeds, preferably wild
0.4%	3.6 g (0.13 oz)	red chile flakes
0.1%	0.91 g (0.03 oz)	freshly ground black pepper
1%	9.1 g (0.32 oz)	minced garlic
1.5%	13.6 g (0.48 oz)	red wine
0.5%	4.5 g (0.16 oz)	red wine vinegar

Whisk together the salt, fennel, chile flakes, and pepper in a small bowl.

Place the pork into a stand mixer bowl, sprinkle with the salt mixture, garlic, wine, and vinegar. Fit onto the mixer with the paddle attachment. Mix on low speed until thoroughly blended and visibly sticky, about 2 minutes.

Raw sausage may be kept tightly sealed in the refrigerator for three to four days or in the freezer for several weeks. Portion bulk sausage into zip-top or vacuum sealer bags and flatten to a thickness of no more than ¾ inch (2 cm) before sealing for speedy freezing and thawing.

Homemade Crème Fraîche and Cultured Butter

YIELDS ABOUT 3 CUPS (705 ML) CRÈME FRAÎCHE OR 11 OUNCES (310 G) OF BUTTER
AND 1½ CUPS (355 ML) BUTTERMILK

The only thing good pasta really needs is good butter and cheese. There's something so fantastic in the simplicity of it. To do it right, cook your pasta until it's very nearly al dente, drain it, and toss it with cold whole butter. This way the emulsion of the butter will stay intact, allowing the raw butter flavor and silky, creamy texture to come through. Top with freshly grated Parmigiano and possibly a grinding of pepper and enjoy. This is one of life's great pleasures!

Use pure pasteurized cream in this recipe. Avoid ultra-pasteurized cream or cream with added thickeners or stabilizers.

1½ pints (710 ml) heavy cream

¼ cup (60 ml) buttermilk or plain kefir

Kosher or sea salt, optional

Blend the cream and buttermilk in a jar, cover with a flour sack towel, and leave at room temperature until thickened, 12 to 24 hours. At this point you have crème fraîche. Crème fraîche will keep for several days tightly sealed in the refrigerator.

To make butter, start with cold crème fraîche straight out of the refrigerator. Whip the crème fraîche in a mixer fitted with a whip attachment on high speed until it just begins to break and look lumpy. Decrease the mixer to low speed to avoid buttermilk splashing everywhere. Continue to mix a few moments longer until there is a clear separation of solid golden butter and liquid white buttermilk.

Drain the butter through a muslin or flour sack towel–lined fine-mesh sieve, reserving the buttermilk for another use. Gather the corners of the muslin together over the butter and squeeze to expel more buttermilk. Transfer the butter to a bowl of ice water and knead using a butter paddle or wooden spoon, replacing the ice water once or twice until it no longer turns cloudy, to rinse away any residual buttermilk as it can shorten the butter's shelf life. Pour off the ice water and continue to knead for a few moments longer to expel any residual water. Season the butter with salt, if desired.

Transfer the butter to a sheet of parchment paper, roll tightly into a thick log, and twist both ends of the parchment paper to seal. Refrigerate until firm. Unsalted butter will keep for several days and salted butter will keep for a couple of weeks tightly sealed in the refrigerator.

Homemade Ricotta

YIELDS 20 OUNCES (565 G) RICOTTA AND A GENEROUS 5 CUPS (1.2 L) WHEY, DEPENDING ON HOW MUCH IT'S DRAINED

Making ricotta is quite easy, and the result has a much better texture and flavor than store-bought. It is rich and creamy, sweet with a hint of tang, and loaded with milky flavor.

Use pure pasteurized milk and cream in this recipe. Avoid ultra-pasteurized milk or cream with added thickeners or stabilizers.

Adjust the moisture content of the ricotta depending on the use. A wetter ricotta is desirable for fresh eating and for garnishing pasta, whereas a dryer ricotta is necessary for pasta and pastry fillings.

The ricotta sets fairly solid in the refrigerator. Bring it to room temperature to use it in recipes—it'll be much easier to mix and spread once the chill comes off of it.

Try this rich and slightly tangy ricotta in ravioli and tortelloni, dollop it over pasta with Simple Tomato Sauce (page 108) or Basil Pesto (page 112), top pizza with it, sweeten it for Cannoli (pages 181-183), or simply enjoy it still warm smeared over good bread and drizzled with olive oil and sprinkled with sea salt.

Whey can be used in braises, baked goods, smoothies, and in Whey Noodles (page 37).

---

1 quart (940 ml) whole milk

1 pint (475 ml) heavy cream

1 pint (475 ml) buttermilk

¼ cup (60 ml) plus 2 tablespoons (30 ml) white vinegar

Combine the milk, cream, and buttermilk in a small, heavy pot. Heat over medium-low heat, stirring once or twice at most, until 200°F (93°C), about 40 minutes. Gently stir in the vinegar, cover, remove from the heat, and let sit until the white curds separate from the watery, translucent yellow whey, about 5 minutes.

Ladle the curds and whey into a muslin or flour sack towel–lined colander set over a large bowl. Gather the corners of the muslin together over the curds and tie with kitchen twine. Let the curds drain until the whey stops dripping, about 2 hours. Squeeze to expel more whey, if desired. On the other hand, if the ricotta turns out too dry for your liking, simply stir a bit of whey back in. Reserve the whey for another use.

Ricotta and whey will keep for several days tightly sealed in the refrigerator.

Homemade Oil-Packed Pickled Peppers

YIELDS ABOUT 1½ QUARTS (1.4 L) PLUS 2¼ CUPS (530 ML) INFUSED VINEGAR

I love the way spicy and tangy pickled peppers perk up all sorts of pasta sauces, but I hate spending $8 for a small jar so I developed this recipe for homemade. It makes a fairly large amount so that you don't have to ration it too carefully. In addition to homemade pasta, it's also delicious on pizzas and in sandwiches, salads, and antipasto platters.

If Fresno chiles are too spicy for you, feel free to substitute all of part of them with additional sweet mini peppers.

The by-product of making this pickled pepper recipe is a brilliant orange spicy infused vinegar. It's great for spiking pasta sauces and soups and in vinaigrettes and coleslaw dressings.

Use the pickled peppers in Cavatelli with Spicy Italian Sausage and Broccoli Raab (page 176).

---

1 lb. (455 g) Fresno chiles, halved, seeded, and cut into chunky slices

2 lb. (910 g) yellow, orange, and red sweet mini peppers, halved, seeded, and cut into chunky slices

14–16 cloves garlic, minced

½ teaspoon dried basil

½ teaspoon dried oregano

2½ teaspoons (12 g) kosher salt

1½ cups (355 ml) cider vinegar

1½ cups (355 ml) white vinegar

1½ cups (355 ml) extra-virgin olive oil

Combine the chiles, peppers, garlic, basil, oregano, salt, cider vinegar, and white vinegar in a large, heavy, nonreactive pot. Bring to a boil and simmer, stirring occasionally, until the peppers are soft and translucent, about 15 minutes.

Transfer the peppers to a fine-mesh sieve and drain, reserving the vinegar for another use. Transfer the peppers to jars and top off with the olive oil.

Refrigerate the peppers for about a week to allow the flavors to marry before use.

Pickled peppers will keep for several months tightly sealed in the refrigerator and the infused vinegar will keep for several months tightly sealed in the pantry.

Crunchy Breadcrumbs

YIELDS ABOUT 3 CUPS (250 G)

Pasta and sauce are almost always soft and tender. Adding something crisp for a textural contrast is a real chef move.

These crumbs are not only a fantastic garnish for pasta dishes, but they're quite tasty in their own right. They're so irresistible in fact that my husband always tries to sneak them as a snack.

8 oz (225 g) artisan-style sourdough bread, cubed

¼ cup (60 ml) extra-virgin olive oil

2 oz (55 g) grated Parmigiano-Reggiano

½ teaspoon granulated garlic

½ teaspoon Hungarian paprika

Generous pinch cayenne pepper

Kosher salt

Freshly ground black pepper

Preheat the oven to 400°F (200°C, or gas mark 6).

Process the bread in food processor until coarse, irregular crumbs form. Transfer to a bowl and toss with olive oil and then the Parmigiano, granulated garlic, paprika, and cayenne until evenly coated. Season with salt and pepper.

Spread the breadcrumbs on a baking sheet and bake until toasted, golden brown, and crisp, about 25 minutes. Let cool to room temperature. Transfer to a jar and cover.

Toasted crumbs will keep for a week or two tightly sealed in the pantry.

Simple Chicken Stock

YIELDS A GENEROUS 3 QUARTS (2.8 L)

This straightforward stock, with its clean chicken flavor and high gelatin content, is versatile enough to go in recipes of any sort, no matter the cuisine. It works in Wonton Soup (page 148) just as well as good old American Chicken Noodle Soup (page 146). You can even doctor it up according to the style of dish you plan to use it in, simmering it with a carrot, a couple of stalks of celery, and a bay leaf for Classic Tortellini (page 65) or a few dried shiitake mushrooms for Shoyu Ramen (page 150).

3 lb. (1360 g) chicken wings

1 large yellow onion, quartered

2 cloves garlic

Kosher salt

Preheat the oven to 425°F (220°C, or gas mark 6).

Roast the chicken wings and onion on a baking sheet until light golden brown, about 1 hour.

Transfer the chicken wings and onion along with any accumulated juice to a large, heavy pot. Add the garlic and 6 quarts (5.7 liters) of water, bring to a boil, and simmer briskly, skimming off any foam that rises to the surface, until reduced by half, about 2 hours. Remove the wings using a skimmer and discard. Strain the stock through a fine-mesh sieve and skim off the fat as desired. Season lightly with salt. Set the container of stock into a large ice bath and stir occasionally to cool as quickly as possible.

Stock will keep for several days in the refrigerator or a couple of months in the freezer.

Simple Beef Stock

YIELDS A GENEROUS 3 QUARTS (2.8 L)

Here's a rich all-purpose beef stock that works in recipes of all sorts, no matter the style or flavor profile. Use it in dishes as diverse as Ragu Bolognese (page 113) and Taiwanese Beef Noodle Soup (page 142).

2 lb. (905 g) meaty beef shanks, 1-inch (2.5-cm)-thick slices

2 lb. (905 g) oxtails, 2-inch (5-cm)-thick slices

1 large yellow onion, quartered

2 cloves garlic

Kosher salt

Preheat the oven to 450°F (230°C, or gas mark 8).

Roast the beef shanks, oxtails, and onion on a baking sheet until dark golden brown, about 50 minutes.

Transfer the shanks, oxtails, and onion along with any accumulated juice and drippings to a large, heavy pot. Add the garlic and 6 quarts (5.7 liters) of water, bring to a boil, and simmer slowly, skimming off any foam that rises to the surface, until reduced by half, about 5 hours. Remove the shanks and oxtails using a skimmer and discard. Strain the stock through a fine-mesh sieve and skim off the fat as desired. Season lightly with salt. Set the container of stock into a large ice bath and stir occasionally to cool as quickly as possible.

Stock will keep for several days in the refrigerator or a couple of months in the freezer.

IMAGINE THE PASTABILITIES: CREATING YOUR OWN NEW PASTAS

Creative and experimental pasta cooks are coming up with fantastic new ideas and also rediscovering old flavors and shapes every day. Once you have a number of batches of pasta under your belt and are comfortable with the basic techniques, you will be able to do the same. You'll learn to make pasta intuitively by feel, almost like an Italian nonna. And then you'll be able to play and create your own unique pasta inventions.

Once you move beyond the recipes, there are endless flavors and a rainbow of colors to explore. Why not try incorporating spices and spice blends, such as pepper or turmeric or perhaps even garam masala? Or add fresh herbs, citrus zest, fruit and vegetable purées, such as carrot, roasted red pepper, roasted garlic, or blueberry? Or perhaps substitute wine, brewed tea, or aquafaba for some of the liquid? Or substitute small amounts of different flours, maybe barley, quinoa flour, or lentil? How about extruding two-toned pasta with your Bigolaro or making variegated cavatelli? Can you imagine stuffed pappardelle or stuffed corzetti, *doppio* ravioli or agnolotti with two fillings, textured farfalle made from stracnar, or shortcutting lorighittas, the painstakingly labor-intensive handmade shape of two intertwined rings from Sardinia, by using freshly extruded spaghetti? Want to grind your own flour to unlock the whole world of flavor of the many varieties of wheat? If you can think of it, you can make it! Imagine all the pastabilities!

SOURCES FOR PASTA MACHINES, OTHER TOOLS AND EQUIPMENT, AND INGREDIENTS

I have personally sourced pasta tools, equipment, and ingredients from the following:

Amazon

amazon.com

All manner of pasta machines and pasta tools, including brass pasta cutters and ravioli stamps (search "La Gondola")

Antica Aguzzeria del Cavallo

aguzzeriadelcavallo.it

All manner of pasta machines and pasta tools, including brass pasta cutters and ravioli stamps and traditional garganelli combs

Arcobaleno

arcobalenollc.com

Prosumer and professional pasta machines, bronze extruder dies, and pasta tools

Artisanal Pasta Tools

artisanalpastatools.com

All manner of pasta tools, including cavarola and other textured pasta boards, corzetti stamps, and rolling pins

Bartolini

bartolinifirenze.it

All manner of pasta machines and pasta tools, including brass pasta cutters and ravioli stamps and traditional garganelli combs

Brian Severson Farms

qualityorganic.com

The most refined buckwheat flour suitable for soba that I have found on the market in the USA.

Carbon Knife Co

carbonknifeco.com

Brass pasta cutters and ravioli stamps

Espresso Coffee Machines

www.ecmcanada.net

Prosumer and professional pasta machines and bronze extruder dies

Fantes

fantes.com

All manner of pasta machines and pasta tools, including exceptional chitarras

◀ All Yolk Tagliatelle

Imaikouba

imaikouba.shop

Textured pasta boards, corzetti stamps, and ravioli molds

PastaArt

etsy.com/shop/pastaart

Sardinian brass pasta wheels

Pastabiz

pastabiz.com

Prosumer and professional pasta machines, including the Bigolaro model B, bronze extruder dies, and pasta tools, including brass pasta cutters and ravioli stamps

Planet Chef

planet-chef.com

Prosumer and professional pasta machines and bronze extruder dies

Repast Supply Co.

repastsupplyco.com

Bigolaro benches (designed in part by yours truly) and ravioli pins

Romagnoli Pasta Tools

romagnolipastatools.com

Corzetti stamps and rolling pins

Sur La Table

surlatable.com

Pasta machines and pasta tools

Tagliapasta.com

tagliapasta.com

All manner of pasta machines and pasta tools, including brass pasta cutters and ravioli stamps

Williams Sonoma

www.williams-sonoma.com

Pasta machines and pasta tools

Wooden Essentials

instagram.com/wooden_essentials

Cavarola and other textured pasta boards, corzetti stamps, and rolling pins (send a DM)

ACKNOWLEDGMENTS

Thank you to my editor Dan Rosenberg for continuing to allow me to write books on the subjects I love.

Thank you to my art director Marissa Giambrone for embracing my aesthetic for the photography.

Thank you to my copy editor Jenna Nelson Patton and project manager Nyle Vialet for both being as nitpicky as I am.

And thank you to the entire crew at Quarto for making this book possible.

Thank you to my husband and taster-in-chief Barry for acting as my Bigolaro-cranking muscle, resident science expert, guinea pig, time taker, scribe, proofreader, barista, DJ, and cheerleader. I couldn't have done this without you and your voracious gotta-make-progress, mountain-riding cyclist appetite.

Thank you to my little brother Andrew for being my collaborator and consultant and brainstorming partner. These recipes are all the more delicious for your contributions.

Thank you to my mom Irina for being my diligent and detail-oriented proofreader.

Thank you to Maja Adiletta and Arcobaleno for providing a Bigolaro extruder die for my use.

Thank you to my friend Melanie Hendry for providing sourdough starter for my use.

Thank you to my friend Laurie Boucher for providing her delicious recipe for lasagna as well as moral support.

Thank you to my friend Tina Prestia for consulting on Italian flour.

ABOUT THE AUTHOR

LUCY VASERFIRER is a culinary educator, chef, recipe developer, food stylist, food photographer, and the author of *Not Your Mother's Cast Iron Skillet Cookbook: More Than 150 Recipes for One-Pan Meals for Any Time of the Day*; *Marinades: The Quick-Fix Way to Turn Everyday Food Into Exceptional Fare, with 400 Recipes*; *Flavored Butters: How to Make Them, Shape Them, and Use Them as Spreads, Toppings, and Sauces*; and *Seared to Perfection: The Simple Art of Sealing in Flavor*. A Le Cordon Bleu graduate with degrees in both culinary arts and patisserie and baking, she lives with her husband in Vancouver, Washington.

Connect with Me on Instagram

Follow me @lucyvaserfirer for more ideas, inspiration, and images of these recipes and the latest episode of Noodlevision. Share your pics using #theultimatepastamachinecookbook. Let's explore the world of pastabilities together!

INDEX